W9-AGK-432

Slippery
TIPPLES

JOSEPH PIERCY

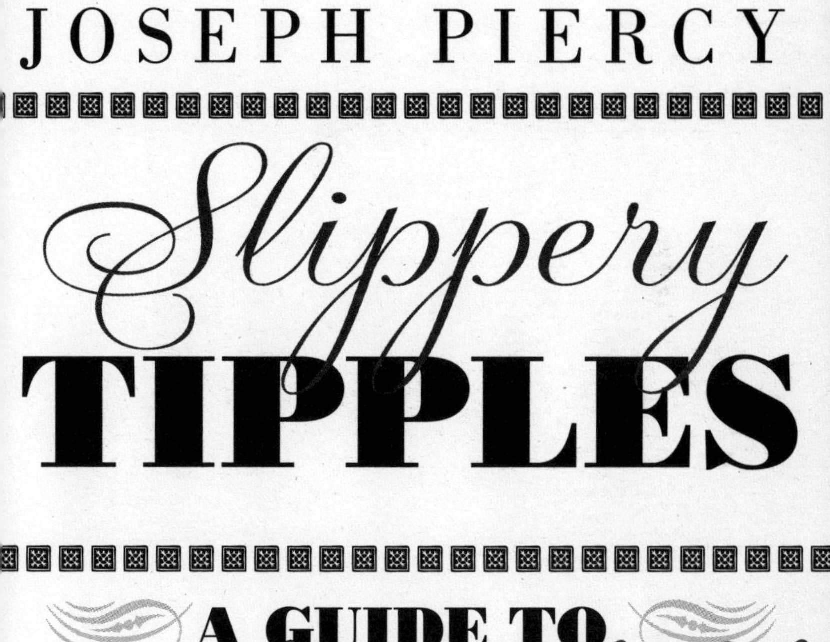

Slippery TIPPLES

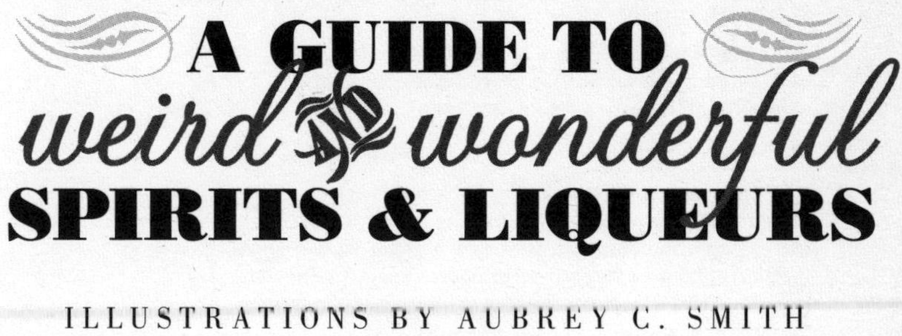

A GUIDE TO *weird and wonderful* SPIRITS & LIQUEURS

ILLUSTRATIONS BY AUBREY C. SMITH

For Joanna and Polly

First published 2010

The History Press
The Mill, Brimscombe Port
Stroud, Gloucestershire, GL5 2QG
www.thehistorypress.co.uk

British Library Cataloguing in Publication Data.
A catalogue record for this book is available from the British Library.

ISBN 978 0 7524 5756 7

Typesetting and origination by The History Press
Printed in Great Britain

CONTENTS

Foreword	6
Austria	11
The Balkans	17
Brazil	24
The Caribbean	28
Chile	33
China	36
Czech Republic	47
Estonia	53
Finland	56
France	61
Germany	84
Greece	94
Hungary	98
India	102
Israel	107
Italy	114
Japan	127
Lithuania	135
Mongolia	138
The Netherlands	142
Norway	147
South Africa	155
Spain	159
United Kingdom	166
United States	177
Appendix: Recipes	181

FOREWORD

Slippery Tipples first started to ferment some years ago in a restaurant in Barcelona. The Catalan capital has a burgeoning reputation as a place of culinary excellence and innovation. New restaurants and designer tapas bars spring up every month and keeping abreast with the latest food fashions is an exhausting, expensive and near-impossible pursuit. The queue to get a seat at the city's hottest table fluctuates on a daily basis and it is easy to be seduced by the hype only to be disappointed by the substance.

As a result of this, one of my favourite places to eat in Barcelona is an unpretentious family-run restaurant in the Born area of the city called Passadis del Pep. A discouraging doorway next to a cash point machine leads into a gloomy corridor with a narrow staircase at the end. The staircase leads down to a large, brightly-lit dining hall, tastefully decorated with abstract paintings adorning the pale walls. However, the feature that caught my eye the first time I dined there was not the decor, pleasant and welcoming though it was, but a large stone inlet lining the back of the room. There, gleaming in the ambient light, was an extraordinary display of hundreds of liqueur and spirit bottles in a myriad of shapes and colours. Assuming it to be the owner's private collection put there for decorative purposes, I sat down and was treated to a parade of courses of excellent locally-caught seafood.

But the reason for this treasure trove of bottles became apparent at the end of the meal. The waiter served coffee and then marched to the back of the room, quickly surveyed the collection and plucked out half a dozen bottles which he brought to the table with shot glasses and invited me to try at my leisure. The contrast between the different drinks was marked and inspiring: sweet fruit liqueurs, herbal digestives and fortified wines, all from different parts of the globe. It transpired that this was a tradition at Passadis del Pep and one which was repeated on every subsequent visit, although I have never been offered the same bottle twice.

It was the experience of dining at Passadis del Pep that first fired my interest in unusual drinks, and on future trips abroad I made it a habit to seek out and sample the local 'hooch'. City breaks to Budapest and Prague yielded the two heavyweights of Eastern Europe, Unicum and Becherovka. My honeymoon on the Amalfi coast in Italy naturally included a visit to a local limoncello factory. A stag weekend in Amsterdam was not spent trawling round the red light district and coffee shops, as might be expected on such unseemly occasions, but on a pilgrimage to the Lucas Bols Genever Museum. Friends and family assisted on my quest and would endeavour to bring back samples from their travels: fearsome Feni from India, sickly sweet Sabra from Israel and a bright blue bottle of 'Hip Hop' Hpnotiq from New York. A chance conversation in the pub led Paul James to raid his father's drinks cabinet for some prizes. The former mayor of Harlow Town, Alex James had been amassing an exquisite and alarming collection of 'Slippery Tipples'. I was duly furnished with some samples of beautifully aged Kruskovac and something mysterious which was, frankly, barely fit for human consumption.

What had started as a hobby, a distraction when travelling or on holiday, was rapidly becoming an obsession. Gradually my interest shifted from a desire to simply taste these weird and wonderful drinks towards exploring and understanding their historical origins and the cultures that they derived from. It was at this point that *Slippery Tipples* began to take shape. Although there were plenty of brightly illustrated guides to spirits and liqueurs available, few seem to explore the historical context and development of the drinks they featured in any depth.

In the course of researching and compiling this guide I developed a theory about the history of modern civilisation. I discovered fascinating areas of history that I had hitherto been entirely ignorant of and realised that in a strange way, I was able to place certain drinks on a timeline against key moments in history. From the golden age of the Tang Dynasty in ancient China and the tragic tale of the concubine Yang Yuhuan, to the Hispanic colonisation of South America, on through the era of the Renaissance to the Ottoman Empire, the spice trade and Industrial Revolution and up to the Second World War; all these key moments in history have a drink attached to them. It may seem trivial to view history through the prism of peculiar alcoholic drinks but at the very least it is a captivating coincidence.

So what, in essence, is a Slippery Tipple and what attributes provide the criteria for inclusion in this guide? Overall there is bias towards fruit- and herb-based liqueurs over spirits (although grain alcohol provides a base for many of the drinks). Many traditional artisanal liqueurs derive from pastoral peasant culture and used ingredients that were easy to forage for and readily to hand. Another key element in what is largely a miscellaneous approach was to select entries that had an interesting historical or cultural background. Lastly, there was some consideration given to how the different entries fared when mixed with other drinks in cocktails or used in food recipes.

One key factor of a Slippery Tipple is that it often tastes much better in situ. Either by dint of getting a little carried away on holiday or falling foul of the charms of local tradesmen skilled at selling to gullible tourists, somehow that delicious local hooch you sampled from the barman you befriended that summer is never quite the same when it is rolled out at a drinks party the following Christmas. The cocktail recipes and culinary suggestions are in the hope that if your ardour for the nectar you have brought back from your travels has waned, it doesn't necessarily have to gather dust in the drinks cabinet or be consigned to the sink.

Slippery Tipples, then, is designed to have two purposes: firstly, to provide both the casual imbiber and liqueur and spirits enthusiast with background knowledge of the ingredients, production techniques and history of some of the world's most unusual drinks; secondly, to offer a subjective account of what to expect from certain drinks from around the world through some light-hearted tasting notes, serving suggestions and general observations of what they may be good for other than getting very drunk.

An appendix has been added to provide recipe information on how to make several approximations/versions of some of the drinks featured and some others that are easy, cheap and fun to produce. The cocktail recipes are derived from a variety of sources; where possible I have tried to credit the creator or mixologist responsible but generally this information is very much in the public domain and many so-called classic cocktail recipes have evolved and changed as drinking habits and fashions have come and gone. The measurements in cocktails are vital in order to maximise the balance of flavours and I have chosen to use 2.5cl as equivalent to one shot. A decent stainless steel cocktail shaker is worth investing in, preferably one with a built-in strainer and a lid that doubles as a measure (medicinal plastic measures are available free from most chemists). Other cocktail accessories such as muddles and stirrers can be improvised with common kitchen utensils. I'm not convinced that there is any need to buy specific cocktail paraphernalia, and I think that double-ended 'Boston style' shakers are for the would-be Tom Cruises of this world.

Time for the dull but necessary word about drinking

responsibly. Over half of the drinks featured in this guide weigh in at over 25 per cent ABV. Some of the cocktails exacerbate their potency when mixed with other liqueurs and spirits and, at risk of appearing a hypocrite, I urge some caution here. Mix these drinks with some moderation and care; some of them have terrifying hangover potential which will severely impair your enjoyment of them after the fact.

I would like to thank the following people for their help, advice and assistance with compiling this guide: Mathew Clayton for his faith and support; Sarah Hale for her input and advice; Gemma Cheney for suggesting the idea in the first place; Giles Coghlin; three times World Mixology Champion Francois Van Iffer; Anthony Page for his kind encouragement; Stuart Small and the regulars at The Newmarket Arms, Brighton; Kal Elhajoui for his additional research; Paul and Alex James; Aubrey C. Smith for his extraordinary drawings; M.S. Lucas; Robin Harries and The History Press for backing the project and my family and friends for putting up with me boring them senseless with long-winded, drink related anecdotes and facts.

Joseph Piercy
Brighton, 2010

AUSTRIA

Altvater/Monopolowa Vodka

DESCRIPTION: Sweet, herb-based liqueur originally produced for medicinal purposes

BACKGROUND: In 1810, Leopold Maximillian Baczewski inherited a small, family-run distillery in Wybranówka, a small suburb of the city of Lwów. (A Polish city since 1349, Lwów had been annexed by the Austrian Empire in 1772 and was incorporated into Ukraine by the USSR in 1939. Its Polish origins notwithstanding, Monopolowa is now manufactured in Austria and it is here that it remains most popular.) Sensing that in order for the business to flourish it needed to be closer to the industrial heart of Lwów, Baczekowski moved the factory into the centre of the city and set about revolutionising the vodka and liqueur distilling business. The main innovation Baczewski introduced was to switch production from the traditional alembic copper stills and embrace Aeneas Coffey's recently invented columnar still, or Coffey, patented in Dublin in 1831.

The advantage of the Coffey was that it allowed the often laborious three-step distillation process to be combined into a one-step method by using three separate interconnected chamber columns. The Coffey produced base alcohol of a much smoother quality containing approximately 90 per cent ABV. It was also considerably safer, as the dangers of producing a base containing poisonous methyl content were greatly reduced. The liqueurs produced proved very popular, not only locally but across the Austrian Empire, so much so that the company was awarded the mark of the Imperial Eagle, a trademark that they were permitted to use on their bottles to distinguish their products as 'Purveyor to Royal and Imperial Court'. The company's most successful product was their double-distilled Monopolowa Vodka, a drink so ubiquitous locally that Baczewski became a separate byword for vodka, suggesting that so superior was its quality that to refer to it merely as vodka was an insult.

The company continued to expand throughout the nineteenth century with branches of the distillery opening in other cities, most notably in Zuckmantal, Silensia under the ownership of Baczewski's brother-in-law Paul Gessler. The Gessler company specialised in the production of a local restorative bitters which they named Altvater. The origins of the recipe for Altvater 'cordial' (medicinal dosage was recommended at three parts Altvater to two parts hot water) are unknown, but its dubious status as a health drink was attested to by many physicians during its heyday. In 1886 Professor Richard Godeffoy, chairman of the influential Imperial and Royal Chemical Laboratory in Vienna, produced a famous paper attesting to the many benefits of Altvater to alleviate discomfort from a myriad of ailments ranging from rheumatoid arthritis to syphilis.

Josef Antoni 'Adam' Baczewski took over the reins of the parent company in the 1870s. A graduate of Lwów University of Technology and an expert in distillation processes, Josef Adam continued the company's aggressive expansion programme. Josef Adam is also regarded as one of the first businessmen to deploy modern marketing techniques to further develop brand awareness, for example, producing limited edition crystal carafes for export markets, printing flyers and leaflets and designing press advertisments. Amongst the many creative stunts Josef Adam implemented was the Baczewski Pavillion, a giant glass carafe-shaped display stand at the Lwów International Trade Fair of 1894.

After over a hundred years of unparalleled success in which the names Baczewski and Gessler had become bywords for spirits and liqueurs of unrivalled excellence, the two arms of the company suffered a dramatic fall from grace during the Second World War. The Lwów headquarters were bombed by the Luftwaffe during the Battle of Lwów in 1939. In the immediate aftermath of the war, the remains were razed to the ground by the Soviet authorities who built a paper mill on the site. Other branches throughout Eastern Europe were either shut down or nationalised and the famous Baczewski brand name ceased to exist.

In Vienna, the Gessler factory suffered a similar fate with its factory ransacked by the advancing Soviet army and production brought to a standstill. Salvation eventually arrived in the form of Paul Gessler's grandson Eduard, who doggedly rebuilt the business and acquired the J.A Baczewski trademark in the combined Altvater Gessler- J.A. Baczewski corporation and reintroduced the revered Monopolowa vodka. The company continues to be overseen by the Gessler and Baczewski families to this day and remains one of Austria's most iconic brands.

TASTING NOTES: As with most central or eastern European herb liqueurs, Altvater is best served ice-cold and downed quickly as a shot. The keynotes are of nutmeg, with a cinnamon blast that provides a pleasing sweetness and a slightly marshmallow-like aftertaste. It is not recommended that you follow Professor Richard Godeffoy's medical advice and dilute it with hot water. This has the effect of unleashing an acrid aroma and as the mixture cools (and given the drink's golden hue) it becomes difficult to escape the unnerving feeling that one is imbibing a urine sample.

GOOD FOR: Monopolowa is a must for anybody who harbours any pretensions of being a vodka fancier. Altvater has a very attractive-looking bottle that at the very least makes the casual observer think one takes the constitution of one's drinks cabinet seriously.

TRIVIA: After the destruction of the Lwów factory in 1945 and the subsequent dissolution of production, Monopolowa became highly sought after by spirits connoisseurs around the world. Vintage bottles dating back to before the war were still being sold at auction up until the early 1980s, fetching thousands of pounds for early-ninteenth-century carafes. The popularity of Monopolowa is credited to the traditional use of potato peelings as the base fermentation crop as opposed to grain bases which are used by most other modern vodkas.

The loss of Monopolowa vodka was deeply felt by the Polish people during the Soviet era. The drink became something of a cause célèbre, with prominent cultural figures such as the dissident poet and playwright Marian Hemar penning odes to its demise. Hemar wrote several comic polka-style tangos in tribute to the wonders of drinking Monopolowa which he performed during his weekly programmes on Radio Free Europe during the 1950s. Hemar eventually settled in Surrey and his remains are buried in a churchyard in Dorking.

Holy Roman Emperor

4cl Altvater
2cl Campari
15cl tonic water
squeeze of lemon
slices of lemon and lime
ice cubes

Named after Francis II, the last of the Holy Roman Emperors and the only *Doppelkaiser* (Emperor of both Austria and Germany simultaneously). Discounting, of course, the claims of a certain Herr Hitler.

Blend the Altvater and Campari in a cocktail shaker (it is advisable to chill the Altvater thoroughly beforehand), pour over ice and top up with tonic, stir, and add a squeeze of lemon and garnish.

Black-Shirted Nazi

4cl Altvater or Jägermeister
15cl Mountain Dew Pitch Black Soda

This offensively-titled cocktail is, at the time of writing, nearly impossible to make as its distinctive black colour depends on the availability of the mixer. Mountain Dew Pitch Black Soda was a limited edition 'energy drink' produced by a subsidiary of Pepsi Cola Incorporated between 2004 and 2005. Various other versions of Mountain Dew are still available but the Pitch Black has been temporarily discontinued. This has led to various internet campaigns and petitions to have it reissued. Pepsi bowed to consumer pressure in 2007 by releasing a limited edition Pitch Black 2, a sour version of the original which proved unpopular with fans of the drink. Bizarrely, Pitch Black's main selling points were that it was made with 'real sugar' and had a very high caffeine content. The cocktail, if indeed it can be called that, is pretty revolting. Imagine, if you can, drinking carbonated, sugar-sweetened squid ink.

THE BALKANS

Kruskovac

DESCRIPTION: Pear-based fruit liqueur popular in the Balkans.

BACKGROUND: Kruskovac hails from the ancient province of Dalmatia on the Adriatic coast, which was initially absorbed into the former state of Yugoslavia but now finds itself spread across Croatia, Bosnia Herzegovina and small areas of Montenegro. Dalmatian cuisine is a strange hybrid of traditional Mediterranean influences from Italy (pastas and risottos) and Spain (cured hams and fresh fish) with the more robust meat stews of Eastern Europe. At the heart of Dalmatian cooking, though, is an obsessive attention to locally sourced ingredients and the Dalmatian pear, which grows in abundance along the Adriatic coast, is held in particular affection by this cultured, if sadly dispossessed people.

Kruskovac is made from a carefully selected distillate of Dalmatian pears and then lovingly matured in oak casks. It has been produced by local farmers in the area for centuries and varies from other pear-based liqueurs on account of its beautiful golden yellow hue. Highly prized by liqueur connoisseurs, kruskovac is fiendishly difficult to get hold of in the UK although the Maraska Company produce an un-aged variety with a milder alcohol content (25 per cent ABV).

TASTING NOTES: One of the drinks of the gods, kruskovac has mild, sweet undertones of vanilla and almonds with a smooth flowery finish. It is one of those drinks that one could easily polish off a bottle of without really noticing. Dangerously quaffable served ice cold in tall glasses with crushed ice and a garnish of fresh torn mint leaves.

GOOD FOR: Culinary experimentation. Simply pour over stewed pears for a bright boozy buzz; alternatively, the stewed pears with kruskovac in thick syrup go well in short crust pastry tartlets. It is also delicious brushed over chicken breasts before grilling or to flambé fruit pancakes.

Traffic Light

An ingenious and near foolproof cocktail that looks mighty impressive.

4cl cherry vodka
4cl kruskovac
4cl Midori

Pour the Midori in first for a green base, then float the kruskovac on top by pouring over the back of a chilled teaspoon. Finally, repeat the floating technique with the cherry vodka and step back and marvel at how clever you are.

Apples 'n' Pears

4cl kruskovac
2.5cl apple flavoured vodka
7.5cl sparkling apple juice
ice cubes

Pour ingredients into a tall glass with ice and stir.

Rakia

DESCRIPTION: Balkan fruit-based liqueur traditionally used in a variety of Slavonic social ceremonies: christenings, weddings and funerals.

BACKGROUND: Rakia is the generic term used to describe fruit based, homemade, brandy. In Serbia and Bulgaria, macerated plums and apricots are most commonly used at the optimum point of ripeness and distilled by gentle boiling in large copper pots. The origins of rakia (or rakija) are uncertain. The Slavs began to spread and settle in the Balkans throughout the sixth and seventh centuries. Historical documentation refers to the popularity and production of a honey-based spirit known as medovača and rakia probably developed through experimentation with the use of different seasonal fruits. Dušan's Code, a kind of Serbian version of the Magna Carta, was presented to and implemented by Tsar Stefan Dušan between 1349 and 1354. Among the mish-mash of early church decrees, common law and ancient Imperial Greek edicts, there is the following passage on the misuse of alcohol which stands as a very early attempt by a state to deal with the seemingly centuries old problem of binge drinking:

> If a drunk goes from somewhere and if provokes or cuts one, or bleeds one, and doesn't kill, to that drunk shall an eye been taken out and a hand cut off. If drunk yells, or takes one's hat off, or embarrass in some other way, and doesn't bleed, that drunk shall be beaten, a hundred times with a stick, then thrown into a dungeon, and then taken out of the dungeon, beaten again, and then let go.
>
> Paragraph 166, Dušan's Code, 1349

By the mid fifteenth century the Ottoman Empire (under the direction of the immodestly titled Suleiman the Magnificent) had captured Belgrade and began importing their own homemade hooch, arak. The name 'rakia' derives from a distortion of the word arak, which in Arabic means sweat and relates to the distillation processes involved in producing spirits. The Ottoman Empire,mindful of the Serbian and Bulgarian penchant for artisanal alcohol, introduced a tax on privately owned stills of 12 akçes (the Ottoman currency).

After the Second Serbian Uprising (1813–1817) made Serbia a semi-independent state, the still tax was lifted and this led to the widespread practice of community distilling that is prevalent in the Balkans to this day.

TASTING NOTES: The quality of rakia varies hugely in accordance with such variables as the fruits and flavourings used, the reliability of the distillation equipment and, most notably, the retail price. For purposes of clarity I shall confine these tasting notes to the plum based rakia of Serbia known as Slivovitz (Šljivovica).

Slivovitz (and rakia in general) has a reputation in Western Europe for being 'Balkan Fire Water' or 'Serbo-Rocket Fuel' and although often the 'straight off the farm' varieties can weigh in at over 60 per cent ABV, commercial producers such as Stefan Nemanja prefer a more modest and palatable 35 per cent ABV. Double distilled and aged in oak casks, Stefan Nemanja has a smoothness that counters the high natural sugar content of the plums. A faint undertone of almonds is provided by the use of toasted and ground plum stones in the fermentation process.

GOOD FOR: Adding a little touch of Eastern European kitsch to weddings, funerals or barmitzvahs (several brands of Slivovitz have been certified kosher). Also works well added to the mixture of traditional Jewish honey and almond flat cakes.

TRIVIA: Rakia has a peculiar relationship with death. In Eastern Orthodox Christian burial services in the Balkans the mourners are directed to the gates of the cemetery at the end of the service. Here they are supplied with a piece of soda or rye bread and a small glass of rakia. The ritual requires the eating of the bread, followed by a sip of rakia. It is then traditional to spill a few drops of rakia on the consecrated ground and to chant in Romanian '*Dumnezeu să-i primească*' (May God receive this for her/him), before finishing the rest of the glass.

Certain writers and artists have played on this relationship between rakia and death. Bram Stoker's protagonist Jonathan Harker is offered Slivovitz whilst travelling to meet Dracula for the first time:

> 'the driver said in excellent German – 'The night is chill, Mein Herr, and my master the Count bade me take all care of you. There is a flask of slivovitz (the plum brandy of the country) underneath the seat, if you should require it.'
>
> *Dracula*, Bram Stoker (1897)

Patricia Highsmith's gentleman serial killer Tom Ripley drinks Slivovitz in Salzburg whilst stalking a man who believes him to be dead in the novel *Ripley Under Ground* (1970).

In the 2006 film *Art School Confidential*, a semi-autobiographical account of comic artist and screenwriter Daniel Clowes' experiences as a student, the principal character Jerome meets Jimmy, a death-obsessed reclusive painter (played by British actor Jim Broadbent) who will only allow people to enter his flat on production of a bottle of Slivovitz.

King Stefan

Named after the twelfth-century medieval ruler of Serbia, Stefan Nemanja (aka Eastern Orthodox Saint, St Simeon who also gives him name to Serbia's best selling brand of Slivovitz).

2cl Slivovitz
4cl blueberry juice
ice

Mix Slivovitz and blueberry juice and pour over crushed ice.

The Serbian Slammer

2cl Slivovitz
2cl sambuca
twist of lime juice

Mix together the ingredients and drink, shooter style.

BRAZIL

Cachaça

DESCRIPTION: Spirit made from raw cane sugar, reminiscent of Caribbean rum which is a comparison, although not wholly accurate, that deeply enrages Brazilians for some reason.

BACKGROUND: The origins of Cachaça date back to the sixteenth century and a period of Brazilian history known as the Sugar Cane Cycle. Attempts by the early Portuguese settlers to mine for gold and silver had proved fruitless and of the fifteen *captancies* (geographical areas of Brazil carved up by King Joắo III) only two remained under effective Portuguese control: Pernambuco and Sắo Vicente. Pernambuco flourished under the proto-governorship of relatively liberal-minded conquistador Duarte Coelho, who established the city of Olinda on Brazil's north-eastern Atlantic coast. Whilst the governors of the other remaining thirteen *captancies* had their hands full roaming round the rainforests, fighting the indigenous population and dealing with the attentions of the French government (who were highly perplexed that Spain and Portugal had divided up the New World cake and not invited them to the party), Duarte Coelho and his counterpart in São Vicente, the explorer Martim Afonso de Sousa, came up with a clever money-making scheme. Duarte Coelho established sugar cane plantations and built large milling factories and for his part, Martim Afonso de Sousa provided African slaves to work the farms and exported the sugar back to Europe.

Duarte Coelho, albeit not very liberal by modern standards given that he ran his colony on repatriated slave labour, nonetheless recognised that keeping his workforce happy considerably aided production. As an incentive, Coelho paid his slaves with the leftover cane juice from the milling process which was distilled by heating in copper pots to produce alcohol or *rhum agricole*. The resulting beverage proved so popular that Coelho and Afonso de Sousa started to exchange the drink now known as Cachaça with African slave traders in order to bolster their work force.

As a result of its humble beginnings, Cachaça was traditionally seen as a peasant's drink, produced by and for the lower classes in Brazil. The fermentation process is relatively easy compared with that of other spirits and liqueurs and this has enabled a do-it-yourself culture to develop, with around 30,000 small producers and micro-distilleries operating in Brazil that produce an astonishing estimated output of 400 million gallons a year for domestic consumption alone (roughly 2.5 gallons per person).

The cane juice is extracted after milling and mixed with maize flour to act as a fermenting agent. The fermentation process takes between 24 and 48 hours before distillation in simple copper stills. Traditionally, this occurs in three distinct phases known as 'the head', 'the heart' and 'the tail'.

'The heart' is extracted and aged mainly in Brazil wood or chestnut barrels (various other woods are also used by different companies) to produce premium gold Cachaça. 'The head' and 'the tail' are bottled immediately after distillation to provide white Cachaça, which although often of dubious quality, is considerably cheaper to purchase.

TASTING NOTES: With so many different companies and home-made varieties available to the domestic market in Brazil, a definitive tasting description is near impossible. Various different woods and aging processes are used, providing subtle distinctions in colour and tone. Due also to a long-running trade dispute with the USA regarding Cachaça's classification, only one per cent of the annual production of the drink is exported. In order to provide a general indicative yardstick, Cabana Cachaça and the Germanic-sounding Weber Haus both provide fine quality versions. Cabana is double-distilled which gives a smoother, less acidic bite. The aroma is one of damp cut grass and dandelion with key notes of mint and honey. Cabana won double gold medals as 'Best in Show White Spirit' at the 2009 San Francisco International Liqueur and Spirit Awards, which represents quite a feat for a product first launched in 2006. Weber Haus produce a variety of different Cachaça for the both the casual drinker and limited edition 'especiales' for the connoisseur. Weber Haus Silver also won a medal at the San Francisco awards; sharper on the palette than the Cabana, the key notes are of mild chilli peppers with a rounded smoky finish.

GOOD FOR: The Caiprinha cocktail, a mix of Cachaça, fresh lime juice and sugar.

Lemon Beat

5cl Cachaça
2tsp runny honey
2.5cl fresh lemon juice
crushed ice

Blend the honey into the Cachaça by stirring in the bottom of a rocks-style whisky glass. Add the fresh lemon juice and fill with crushed ice.

Caiprinha

5cl Cachaça
2.5cl sugar syrup
1 lime cut into wedges
crushed ice

Use a wooden muddle or pestle and bash the limes with the sugar syrup to release the juices. Add the Cachaça and crushed ice.

THE CARIBBEAN

Blue Curaçao

DESCRIPTION: A bittersweet orange liqueur made from laraha fruit to which Dutch liqueur giants Lucas Bols added artificial blue colouring.

BACKGROUND: The origin of Blue Curaçao is a matter of considerable historical debate with various producers and brands laying claim to being the original. Beyond dispute, however, is the country and circumstances from which the drink is derived. The small southern Caribbean island of Curaçao was discovered by Spanish explorers in 1499. Under the leadership of Alonso de Ojeda, a former protégé of Christopher Columbus and by all accounts a man with a spiteful and vindictive temperament, virtually all of the native inhabitants of the island were rounded up and deported to other Spanish colonies to be used as slaves. Soon afterwards the Spanish set up a small colony on the island with the idea of using the land to grow Valencia oranges. Unfortunately, a combination of dry, barren, mineral-free soil and the unpredictable climate resulted in the production of oranges too small and bitter tasting for general consumption. Disappointed that their crops had failed the Spanish abandoned the island, leaving the orange trees to grow wild.

In 1634 the Dutch colonised Curaçao realising that, despite lacking the resources and treasures sought in other parts of the New World, it be of commercial use to slave traders. The Dutch West India Company set up the capital Willemstad and developed it as one of the main trading posts for slaves brought in from Africa. Lucas Bols, owner of the Amsterdam-based distillery firm, held considerable shares in the Dutch West India Company and its East Indian counterpart, largely to ensure the cheap supply of spices for the production of their drinks. At some point, the question of what to do with the wild bitter oranges growing on the island (known to the locals as laraha trees) must have surfaced and the discovery was made that by drying the under-ripe peel of the fruit a fragrant, etheric oil could be extracted. Bols maintain that this bitter orange flavoured oil was exported back to Amsterdam and used in the development of a drink which closely resembles the Blue Curaçao used in numerous cocktails today. Quite where, when, or why the blue colouring was added to an otherwise colourless liqueur remains a mystery. Lucas Bols was fond of adding an element of alchemical mystery to his products and so it is likely that the colouring was added to provide an element of exotic chic (*see* **Hpnotiq**).

An alternative history of the drink (although it concurs with the failed Valencia oranges theory) is proposed by the Senior Company, based on the island. A prominent Jewish family, the Seniors, claim to have come across an 'original' recipe for the drink in 1896 and set up production. As Senior are currently the only producer who harvest and use lahara fruits from the island of Curaçao, the Alcohol and Tobacco Tax Division of the United States have ruled that Senior's is the only Curaçao permitted to put the word 'authentic' on its label.

The production of Senior's 'Curaçao of Curaçao' is pleasingly artisanal. The company has a small plantation of around forty-five ancient trees producing roughly 200 fruits each per year. The harvest is undertaken by hand-picking the fruit when still green (if the peel becomes two thin the fragrant oil is affected) from atop specially designed wooden ladders, cutting the peel with wooden knives and leaving it to dry in the sun for up to five days. The peel is then hung in muslin-like 'jute' bags inside the Senior family's original 100-year-old copper still and left to infuse a mixture of alcohol and water. Additional secret spices and ingredients (blue food colouring anyone?) are added after four to five days and left to ferment for a further two days before bottling.

TASTING NOTES: Although originally designed as an aperitif, the sweet bitterness of the laraha peel can be a little too tart for most palettes. Where Blue Curaçao really excels, though, is in combination with other drinks in cocktails. The sharp, acidic citrus after notes perfectly compliment sweeter sugary mixers such as pineapple juice and creme cassis. It also turns almost any concoction attractive shades of blue or green.

GOOD FOR: Hawaiian-themed barbeques or parties. Make up a sizeable punch bowl of Blue Hawaii, garnish liberally with chopped cherries and slices of fresh pineapple and when the party is in full swing, suggest an impromptu limbo competition.

TRIVIA: The most famous of the many cocktails containing Blue Curaçao is the Blue Hawaii (*see* recipe below) which is generally considered to be named after the Elvis Presley film of the same name. However, the cocktail predates the film of sun, surf, sand and trying to avoid the nagging attentions of a hectoring mother (played by 35-year-old Angela Lansbury when Presley himself was just 27!) by four years. Harry Yee, legendary barman at the Hilton Hawaiian Village Hotel in Waikiki was asked by a sales representative of Lucas Bols to derive a cocktail to boost sales and after some experimenting hit upon the definitive blue drink in a tall glass.

Blue Curaçao is peculiarly popular with singer/songwriters: Joni Mitchell, Lou Reed and Jack Johnson all name-check the drink in a variety of laments. Perhaps due to the ease with which Curaçao rhymes with 'oh' and 'go'. More recently cult indie singer Christopher Browden (*Mansions*) bucked the trend with his song *Curaçao Blue* which contains the lines:

> I know just what I was drinking when I first was untrue
> sea air, cheap beer, and some loneliness
> all mixed with curaçao blue

Classic Harry Yee Blue Hawaii

2.5cl light rum
4cl pineapple juice
2.5cl Blue Curaçao
2.5cl cream of coconut
1 slice of pineapple
1 cherry

Blend the light rum, Blue Curaçao, pineapple juice, and cream of coconut with one cup of ice in an electric blender at high speed. Pour contents into a highball glass. Decorate with the slice of pineapple and a cherry.

Liquid Cocaine

2.5cl vodka
2.5cl Blue Curaçao
1cl lime juice

Measure and stir over ice, drink as a shooter.

Chicha

DESCRIPTION: Home-made beer-like moonshine made from maize and/or cassava or a variety of different available fruits.

BACKGROUND: 'Chicha' is a generic term used across Spanish speaking countries of South America for almost any type of fermented drink. The most commonly-used base ingredient is a type of maize grain known as *Jora*, hence the full name of *Chicha de Jora*. The production of maize-based alcohol originates from the great Inca Empire of the fifteenth and early-sixteenth centuries which colonised large swathes of South America, from Peru and Ecuador down to areas of northern Argentina and Chile.

Incan society set great store by education and the imparting of knowledge and skills to the population. An elaborate caste system existed, with the higher echelons educated directly by the *Amautas*, an elite of philosophers, poets, artists and mystics. The Amautas, from their seat of power in Cusco, Peru, dispatched agents to the different regions of the federation to hand-pick promising students for instruction by the elders so that they in turn could impart this learning to the people. An enlightened development was the creation of the *Acllahuasis*, schools created specifically for young women. Alongside the usual instruction in Inca lore, students chosen to attend the *Acllahuasis* were taught traditional skills such as textile work, ceramics and the brewing of chicha.

The preparation of the Inca *chicha de jora* involved the careful germination of maize to extract the malt sugars and natural starches. To this end, the maize was roughly ground and then moistened in the maker's mouth with saliva, then spat out into ceramic pots and formed into flat discs which were dried in the sun. The wort discs were then macerated and boiled in huge earthenware pots before being left to ferment for several days. The theory of the chewing is based on the use of the diastase enzymes in human saliva to break down the maize and release the maltose, quite literally 'spitting in the beer'.

The other common type of chicha is an unfermented version made with ears of purple corn (*choclo morado*), pineapple rind, cinnamon and cloves known as *chicha morado*.

TASTING NOTES: The colour of chicha varies according to the length of fermentation. Young *chicha de jora* has a milky yellowish brown appearance with a slightly sour aftertaste reminiscent of English 'scrumpy' cider. The colouring becomes paler as the fermentation period is increased and some chicha-makers believe that leaving it in darkened surroundings aids maturation and increases strength. It contains a slight amount of alcohol, 1–3.5 per cent ABV.

GOOD FOR: *Chicha de jora* is excellent in a traditional Peruvian dish of spiced stewed goat (*Seco de Cabrito*). Marinate the kid goat meat with crushed garlic cloves, coriander and chilli paste and add a hearty glass of chicha for at least four hours before adding stock and root vegetables and slow cooking over a low heat until the meat is tender.

TRIVIA: *Chicha morado*, due largely to the supposed 'super food' properties of purple corn, is believed to be good for lowering blood pressure. Historians studying the Inca Empire believe that chicha could have been brewed for medicinal purposes and point to recent research that posits the theory that *chicha de jora* can act as an anti-inflamatory on the prostate gland. Remnants of what appears to be large milling equipment have been unearthed at Machu Pichcu which suggests that chicha was made in large quantities for use in symbolic feasts and festivals. The existence of mills has also been seized upon by academics who maintain that Macchu Picchu was not built as a giant holy temple at all, but as an industrial and agricultural complex.

COCKTAIL RECIPES

As Chicha is, at base level, South American home-brewed corn beer, it doesn't lend itself particularly well to mixing with other drinks. However, the sourness can be lightened by mixing shandy-style with lemonade or lime cordial. A simple recipe for making *Chicha de jora* is included in the recipe appendix.

CHINA

Du Kang

DESCRIPTION: Ancient wheat-based distillate drunk ceremonially at traditional Chinese social gatherings.

BACKGROUND: Chinese folk legends tell of the peasant boy named Du Kang who lived during the Xhou Dynasty (256–11 BC) as the creator of China's most popular liqueur. Born into the family that held office in the Imperial Court, Du Kang's life was one of hardship and misfortune. His father was implicated in a plot against the emperor and, along with Du Kang's mother and brothers, was put to death. Du Kang and his uncle managed to escape and disguised themselves as peasants to avoid detection by the imperial guards. After wandering the country as beggars, Du Kang and his uncle made a camp by a natural spring in the mountains. They were discovered by the local landowner who blackmailed them into working for him in return for not turning them over to the authorities. They worked long hours for very little food and after some time Du Kang's uncle fell ill from malnourishment. In order to help his uncle, Du Kang would save half of his wheat and millet ration and hide it in a hole in a tree near to the mountain spring. At harvest time, the landowner sent Du Kang and his uncle away to the plains to help with harvesting the crops and when they returned to their mountain camp some weeks later, Du Kang discovered that the wheat rations he had left behind had been transformed. Putting his hand into the hole in the tree, he pulled out a lump of sticky yellowish mush which when squeezed through his fingers produced a fine golden liquid. On tasting the liquid, Du Kang and his uncle's fortunes were transformed. They escaped from the landowner to a small village in northern China and set up a workshop to produce their drink, distilling wheat and millet through steamed water and trading their product with locals. Taking the name of its inventor, the drink rapidly became very popular and its fame spread across China. The great warlord and poet Cao Cao, a grand chancellor of the Han Dynasty (AD 155–220) was much taken with the drink and is attributed with a quote that adorns the walls of many bars and restaurants to this day: 'What can cure my melancholy? Du Kang of course!'

TASTING NOTES: The legend of Du Kang tells of the peasant boy being drawn to discover his creation by a sweet aroma. Three thousand years on it is hard to imagine anybody being drawn to a glass of Du Kang by an aroma which is unquestionably reminiscent of diesel. The clear, watery yellowish liquid can also be something of a turn-off for obvious reasons. However, Du Kang is not a drink to be sipped and savoured. On the contrary, tradition dictates that imbibing it be done as swiftly and as clinically as possible.

This is just as well since, with an ABV of 50–60 per cent, it has a furnace-like after-burn that can last on the palette for several, seemingly endless, excruciating minutes.

GOOD FOR: Given its considerable reputation as one of the world's fiercest fire waters, a quick bout of Du Kang toasting can be relied upon to lower the macho bravado of the most belligerent drinker.

TRIVIA: Du Kang is not traditionally taken as either an *aperitif* or a *digestif* but drunk during Chinese family or social feasts. A small, usually ornate, shot glass is placed next to each diner. The host sits at the head of the table and periodically fills his guests' glasses and proposes a toast. According to traditional etiquette, guests show respect to their elders by ensuring that when they chink glasses, they hold their glass lower to observe their status. Guests of a lower social caste or standing are also required to stand up after the toast and deliver a short grovelling apology to the other diners (a peculiar anomally in a Maoist state where all subjects are, notionally at least, deemed to be equal). This process is repeated frequently throughout the feast until, inevitably, all of the guests are well-oiled, unconscious and/or violently sick. A final toast is then proposed to the host who can consider a job well done.

There are numerous references to the imbibing of Du Kang in ancient Chinese poetry. In the modern era, post-modernist Scottish poet Frank Kuppener's two volumes of Chinese free-verse quatrains 'A Bad Day for the Sung Dynasty' and 'The Second Best Moment in Chinese History' are dedicated in part to the traditions of drinking Du Kang.

COCKTAIL RECIPES

There is very little tradition of before- or after-dinner drinking in China and almost no tradition of mixing drinks in cocktail form. The Chinese approach to imbibing alcohol, though steeped in ceremony, is ruthlessly efficient: they get it down their necks as swiftly as possible. The following recipe is for the Chinese equivalent of a summer 'fruit cup' and is notable for its high alcohol content. The Chinese clearly take their drinking very seriously.

Yellow Crystal

60ml fresh orange juice
20ml rice wine
100ml Du Kang
140ml water with a little bicarbonate of soda dissolved into it (about 1/3 tsp)
chopped mint and fresh lychees
handful of ice cubes

Combine all the liquid ingredients together in a large jug (500ml) and leave chilling overnight to meld the flavours. Serve in tall glasses garnished with the mint and chopped lychees. I haven't been able to discover why the baking powder is strictly necessary – possibly it adds an extra tone or aids fermentation.

Ly Shan

DESCRIPTION: Fruit based liqueur made from lychees and rose petals.

BACKGROUND: The origin of the name for this mild, sweet, beautifully coloured fruit liqueur is richly steeped in Chinese folklore. During the heady 'Golden Age' of the Tang Dynasty (AD 618–907), generally considered to be the cultural pinnacle of Chinese civilisation, Emperor Xuanxong is said to have become completely besotted with one of the young palace concubines Consort Yang Yuhuan, whom he would spy on bathing every morning.

Unfortunately for the emperor, Yang Yuhuan belonged to his son Li Mao, the Prince of Shou. Undeterred by the awkward problem of being uncontrollably infatuated with his own daughter-in-law, Xuanxong simply found a new wife for his son and elevated Yang Yuhuan to the position of Yang Guifei, the highest possible position for a concubine. In order to avoid the obvious scandal involved in taking girl who was, to all intents and purposes, a low-ranking servant and making her the proto-empress of Imperial China, Xuanxong also promoted members of Yang Yuhuan's family to positions of power and influence in the imperial court.

Historical opinion is divided as to nature of Yang Yuhuan's character. On one hand, she is depicted in classical Chinese art as one of 'The Four Beauties': women of goddess-like stature whose virtues, grace and physical splendour brought powerful emperors and empires to their knees. On the other, tales of her terrible tantrums, vanity and obsessive self-promotion suggest she was the Tang dynasty's equivalent of Katie Price. Chinese literature tells of her being afflicted with monstrous and overpowering body odour which led to an obsession with bathing and producing scented powders and perfumes. Ever willing to please his favourite concubine, the emperor detailed an army of 700 men to scour the countryside collecting flowers, lychees and other fruits for Yang Yuhuan to use in her ever expanding range of beauty products. Yang Yuhuan is said to have been particularly fond of lychees and rose petals and thus is credited with creating Ly Shan, although not as an after dinner *digestif*, as it is drunk today, but most likely as a bath oil.

Yang Yuhuan's life came to an ignominious end during the Anshi rebellion of AD 755. Her influence over the emperor had enabled her to promote the career of her second cousin, Yang Guozhong, to head of the military. Unfortunately, Yang Guozhong proved to be something of a loose canon with an unerring ability to rub powerful Chinese warlords up the wrong way. One such warlord, An Lushan (whom it was rumoured was having an illicit affair with Yang Yuhuan) declared war on the imperial court, causing huge civil unrest. The imperial guards threatened to mutiny unless Yang Yuhuan was put to death as they blamed her championing of Yang Guozang for causing the uprising. At first the emperor refused but, realising he had little choice, instructed one of his eunuchs to take his beloved to a Buddhist shrine outside of the city walls where she was strangled and buried in an unmarked grave. Emperor Xuanxong was wracked with guilt and remorse for betraying his true love, and went with the eunuch to dig up her body only to find all trace of her remains had disappeared and rose bushes growing where her grave should have been. The emperor sunk into incurable melancholy and died soon afterwards of a broken heart.

TASTING NOTES: Ly Shan is sweet, but much smoother than many other fruit liqueurs on account of its relatively modest alcohol content (16 per cent ABV). Drunk neat, preferably slightly chilled, the slightly bitter/sour undertones of the lychees are prominent with a faint flowery finish of the rose petals.

GOOD FOR: Evoking the majesty and decadence of ancient Imperial China. Run yourself a hot bath of fragrant essential oils, mix up a Silver Palace cocktail (see recipe below) and, slipping indolently into the water with drink in hand, allow yourself to drift into a reverent dream of the simpering beauty and unctuous odours of the concubine Yang Yuhuan.

TRIVIA: The story of Yuag Yuhuan is immortalised in 'The Song of Everlasting Sorrow' an epic poem by Bai Juyi (AD 772–846) in which the Emperor persuades a Taoist mystic to raise the ghost of his lost love only for her to issue the following curse in the poems last lines:

> Even the heaven and earth has their ending times,
> The regret of our parting will last forever and never end.

Chinese Acrobat

4cl Mescal Tequila
2cl Ly Shan
10cl orange juice
4cl kumquat juice
2cl kiwi fruit liqueur (eg Joseph Cartron)
slices of kiwi fruit to garnish

Put the ingredients into a cocktail shaker with some crushed ice, shake well, pour into a high glass and garnish with slices of fresh kiwi. It is advisable not to attempt anything too acrobatic after drinking this cocktail.

Silver Palace

4cl Japanese saki or rice wine
2cl Ly Shan
4 peeled and pitted lychees
1 tsp of runny honey
pomegranate seeds

Put the fruit and liquid into a food blender and mix well (add a little more Ly Shan if the mixture becomes a little viscous). Pour into a cocktail glass and garnish with a sprinkling of pomegranate seeds.

Maotai

DESCRIPTION: China's 'official' national drink made from fermented sorghum grasses.

BACKGROUND: Maotai originated in the heyday of the Quig Dynasty in the eighteenth century. The last great imperial civilisation of China set great store by the creation of a cultural history which was planned to last for thousands of years. Amongst the many programmes the Quig Dynasty instigated was the creation and development of the science of wine making. To this end a centre of excellence was created in a small suburban town on the outskirts of the city of Renhuai, known as Maotai.

The town of Maotai, in the Guizhou province of south-western China, is renowned for its unique microclimate and vegetation which is particularly conducive to the farming of sorghum, a species of maize-like wild grass that resembles green pampas. The sorghum is milled and fermented in water from the nearby River Chisui, which is believed by locals to contain mystical properties. In the 1970s, the Chinese authorities became mindful of the supply of the nation's favourite drink (which is produced by the state-controlled Kweichow Company) and set up a large factory complex in the nearby town of Zunyi. The factory failed spectacularly, despite meticulous replication of the brewing techniques, and this has led to the theory that only wine produced from Maotai can reach the required levels of quality control.

The Kwiechow Company takes up over two-thirds of the town, with the final third given over to small, cottage producers of different varieties of sorghum wine. Not surprisingly, virtually the entire adult population of Maotai is involved in some capacity with the production and distribution of the wine. The techniques behind the production of Maotai are extremely secretive and despite attempts to industrialise the process, large parts of the labour are still undertaken by hand. One of the key elements in the process is the cultivation of a rare type of wheat yeast called jiuqu which is added to the river water and sorghum and left to ferment at high temperature in giant open vats the size of a small swimming pool. Maotai is then distilled and re-distilled a total of nine times before being left to age and then finally bottled.

As a result of the meticulous and time-consuming processes the annual production of Maotai pre-1958 rarely rose above an average of 600 tons. Given the mind boggling size of the Chinese population this minimal output led to the wine becoming scarce in other parts of the country and as a result highly prized.

Chairman Mao Zedong is believed to have visited Maotai in 1958 and demanded that production be increased to 10,000 tons per annum as part of the modernisation programmes of the much vaulted 'cultural revolution'. Unwilling to sacrifice centuries of tradition for a cheaper and inferior product, the people of Maotai resisted Mao's request and it wasn't until 2006 that the Kweichow Company's annual output reached the level that the authorities had targeted almost 40 years before.

TASTING NOTES: Maotai is traditionally served slightly above room temperature which does its slightly off-putting musky aroma no favours whatsoever. Maotai connoisseurs talk of the silky, syrup like smoothness of the drink, especially the premium aged varieties (which can weigh in at an impressive 54 per cent ABV). However, despite some faint caramel undertones it is very hard to escape the sensation of drinking luke-warm soy sauce.

GOOD FOR: Splashing over noodle dishes for a slightly boozy kick or adding to a mixture of soy sauce and sweet chilli relish to make a dipping sauce for dim sum.

TRIVIA: Maotai is the official national drink of the People's Republic of China and as such is the only alcohol that is ever served in Chinese embassies around the world. Richard Nixon was believed to be a fan of Maotai after allegedly getting drunk on it with Chairman Zhou Enlai during a landmark state visit to China in 1972.

COCKTAIL RECIPES

There is no tradition of mixing alcoholic drinks into cocktails in China and such is the popularity and almost sacred status Maotai holds amongst the Chinese people it would be considered an offence to do so. It is also very hard to comprehend of any other flavours to marry it with.

CZECH REPUBLIC

Becherovka

DESCRIPTION: Herb-based liqueur derived from a medicinal recipe traditionally sipped as a side accompaniment to beer.

BACKGROUND: The dreamy city of Karlovy Vary (Carlsbad) had a blossoming reputation as a place of healing, rest and recuperation when in 1794 the 15-year-old Josef Becher opened a small shop, *U tří skřivanů* (At The Three Skylarks) to trade spices and herbal remedies with the passing aristocratic tourists. Karlovy Vary had been a spa town since the fourteenth century when Holy Roman Emperor Charles IV conferred special privileges upon the city after bathing in the hot springs. Keen to cash in on the constant stream of European royalty passing through the town, Josef set about experimenting with distilling herbal mixtures to create restorative bitters. Becher's big break came through a chance encounter with the personal physician of Count Maximillian Friedrich von Plettenberg-Wittem-Mietingen (the Holy Roman Empire liked the nobility to have lengthy names), a somewhat shady Englishman known simply as Doctor Frobrig.

Very little is known about Doctor Frobrig's background or where he learned the art of distilling. A personal physician was a must-have member of any aristocratic entourage in the eighteenth and ninteenth centuries and an ability to concoct spurious quack medicine a key part of the job description. Nonetheless, it is Frobrig who is credited with passing on the know-how to Josef Becher to produce an indigestion recipe that he subsequently sold in his shop under the name of 'English Bitters'. Josef Becher's bitters became very popular with tourists to Karlovy Vary and soon attracted the attentions of *Dopplekaiser* Francis II, who placed a standing order for fifty litres a month to be distributed amongst the members of the Viennese court. Such was the popularity of Becher's digestion remedy it afforded its creator all the trappings of local celebrity. He was able to establish and expand his business, dabble in local politics (he stood as mayor and privy councillor of Karlovy Vary) and father an astonishing sixteen children by various women. Josef Becher's notoriety as a womaniser maybe accounts for the urban myth that Becherovka has aphrodisiac qualities.

Shortly before Josef's death in 1840, his son Jan Becher took over the running of the family business at The Three Skylarks. Jan changed the name to Becherovka, built a new factory to deal with increased demand and a burgeoning export business and commissioned a local glassblower to design the famous flat-fronted bottle (although the distinctive dark-green glass was not introduced until 1907).

Becherovka was supplied as part of the basic rations to soldiers serving on the front during both the first and second world wars and was finally introduced to the United Kingdom by Lord Walter Runciman in 1938. Prime Minister Neville Chamberlain, as part of his policy of appeasement, dispatched Lord Runciman to broker negotiations between the the Third Reich and the Czechoslovakian government over the disputed Sudetenland. According to some historical sources (most notably Maria Dowlings's *Czechoslovakia* (2002)), Runicman spent most of the time being heartily wined and dined by influential aristocratic Germans who duly poured large quantities of Becherovka down his neck. One particularly fraught summit meeting is rumoured to have taken place in the cellars of the Becherovka factory itself. Not surprisingly, Lord Runciman developed quite a penchant for the drink and set about importing it for sale in various London gentlemen's clubs.

The last member of the Becher family and the only woman to hold the company reins was Hedda Becher. Sadly for Hedda, the post-war communist era saw the company fall under state control. Hedda herself, although of an established Bohemian background, fell foul of the mass expulsions of Sudetan Germans from Czechoslovakia. Anti-German sentiment was rife in the post-war period and Becherovka's role in the Runciman negotiations can scarcely have helped her cause. Hedda did however set up a new Becherovka company in exile producing an approximate version (Dr Frobrig's recipe had been requisitioned by the communist authorities) and this led to the drink being produced with two separate labels. Surprisingly, Becherovka continued to flourish under communism, despite state sanctions on export limitations. Hedda was able to return to Karlovy Vary after the 1989 revolution and the process of privatising the Becherovka company began in the 1990s. Becherovka is now largely owned by the drinks giant Pernod-Ricard with a small share, for posterity's sake, still held by the Czech state.

TASTING NOTES: Becherovka forms part of a triumvirate of Central European herb liqueurs along with Unicum and Jägermeister. All three vary in sweetness and tone but they share a similar palette-stripping after-taste. Cinnamon provides the key notes with a bitter dark chocolate undertone. Traditionally, Becherovka is to be sipped and savoured accompanied by Czech Pilsner beer but the sipping approach seems to heighten the acidic after-taste so downing it shot style and using the beer as a chaser is highly recommended.

GOOD FOR: The 'Beethoven' drinking game much beloved by gurgling frat boys on American university campuses. Basically, rent a copy of any one of the *Beethoven* films (schlocky 'family' films about an uncontrollable St Bernard dog) and take a shot of Becherovka every time the dog does something daft. The rules can be expanded or amended to suit the participants.

TRIVIA: Amongst the usual parade of Europe's trendiest courtiers, Karlovy Vary also became a favourite retreat for other nineteenth-century celebrities. Johann Wolfgang Goethe is known to have made regular visits to the city to 'take the waters' and, despite being an avowed teetotaller, records in his diary of July 1812 purchasing a bottle of the locally produced digestive 'bitters'. Ludwig Van Beethoven, who would often accompany Goethe on a 'walkabout' through Karlovy Vary's cobbled streets (much to the delight of the locals) was also known to imbibe large quantities of Becherovka on recuperative trips to the city. Beethoven's drinking is a thorny subject for classical music scholars with several recent books claiming he died of internal organ failure brought on by alcoholism and not a long battle with hepatitis (amongst other ailments). There is no evidence, however, that excessive consumption of Becherovka causes deafness.

Red Moon

4cl Becherovka
15cl cranberry juice
5cl soda water
slice of orange

Pour Becherovka and cranberry juice over ice, stir and top up with soda. Garnish with the orange.

Sun Festival

4cl Becherovka
4cl dark rum
2cl Amaretto Ramazzotti
15cl pineapple juice
2cl lemon juice
5cl soda water
1 tsp sugar

Blend ingredients by stirring into a cocktail shaker with ice, shake gently and strain into a tall glass.

ESTONIA

Vana Tallinn

DESCRIPTION: Sweet spiced liqueur with rum-like undertones, usually drunk with desert or coffee.

BACKGROUND: Prior to the break-up of the Soviet Union, Vana Tallinn was one of Eastern Europe's best kept secrets. Produced largely for the domestic market and the neighbouring Baltic States, Vana Tallinn dates back to the early 1960s when Liviko, traditionally a producer of cheap, low-grade vodka, branched out into the liqueur market. The result was an instant success and Vana Tallinn quickly established itself as the national drink of Estonia, rivalling the Soviet-endorsed hegemony of vodka.

The drink is a careful merging of root alcohol, infused citrus oils and spices blended with Jamaican rum. Since the break up of the Soviet Union, Vana Tallinn, and in particular the Liviko distillery, have been gradually building a worldwide reputation which has culminated in a series of high profile awards, most notably the silver medal at the San Francisco World Spirits Expo of 2008.

TASTING NOTES: Vana Tallinn is produced in various different versions, differentiated mainly by their alcohol content which ranges from 40 per cent ABV to 50 per cent for the special reserve. In terms of taste there is little difference apart from the rum undertones, which are more prevalent in the stronger versions. An initial burst of sugary sweetness of chest-warming rum gives way to hints of vanilla and cinnamon and a slightly tart, citrus finish. There is also a cream liqueur version which, sadly, is pretty revolting and tastes like somebody has poured a shot of rum into a can of condensed milk and left it lying around in the sun for a few days.

GOOD FOR: Chatting up Eastern European foreign students from the Baltic States. There isn't much Tallinn is noted for other than an enormous choral song festival held every five years where up to 300,000 people gather to get drunk and sing folk hymns.

TRIVIA: The beautifully preserved medieval city of Tallinn, with its sawdust-strewn cellar bars and narrow cobbled streets has recently started to fall foul of the curse of the low-cost airline and its cargo of leery, priapismic stag parties. Cheaper than Prague or Barcelona (where the locals rightly view beery weekend revellers with the contempt they deserve), Tallinn has a lot going for it, not least that the local population actually seem to quite enjoy being invaded by drunken neanderthals. Liviko have been known to place sprightly blond personality girls at the airport to accost groups of western European tourists with goodie bags of Vana Tallinn miniatures and merchandising to ensure that when they get drunk they at least get drunk on the city's favourite liqueur.

Hammer and Sickle

2cl Vana Tallinn
8cl sparkling wine

Known originally as the Hammer and Sickle (in the post Soviet era it has been renamed 'The Tickle Tickle') because it 'bashes you over the head and then cuts off your legs'. This is a dangerously quaffable cocktail if made with good quality sparkling wine. For the authentic touch though, it really should be made with Georgian or Russian *Champanski* (she of the saccharine lips with bubbles like air-borne dirigibles).

Limbo

2.5cl Vana Tallinn
4cl lemon flavoured vodka (Absolut or Limonaya)
8cl pineapple juice
juice of half a lemon

Pour all the ingredients over ice and mix with a swizzle for a sunny Caribbean twist to this very Eastern European drink.

FINLAND

Lakka

DESCRIPTION: A fruit flavoured brandy-style liqueur made from wild cloud berries.

BACKGROUND: It is hard to think of any European country which, throughout its history, has had a relationship with alcohol as problematic as Finland's. Whilst the rest of Europe was merrily experimenting, developing and producing all manner of wild and wonderful beverages, Finland always displayed a pious reticence when it comes to the demon drink.

As early as 1775, the Finnish authorities began establishing strict controls over the production and consumption of alcohol by making the practice of distilling a matter of royal privilege and outlawing the ownership and operation of private stills. This 'Royal Privilege' effectively enabled the autocratic king of Sweden, Gustave III (Finland was under the control of the Swedish monarchy between the twelfth and early ninteenth centuries) to be the sole producer of spirits. Gustave III had utter contempt for anything remotely resembling progressive social values of liberty and fraternity, preferring instead to invoke his 'divine' right as king to do pretty much as he pleased. Alongside his avid interest in the arts and especially theatre and opera, Gustave was also something of a gourmet who was renowned for throwing elaborate and decadent banquets. Gustave commissioned a royal distillery to be built in Kuopio, Koljonniemi, in 1783, presumably to develop drinks for himself and his invited guests. Gustave had little time to enjoy his private drinks distillery though; he was assassinated at a masked ball in 1792 by a cabal of disgruntled Swedish noblemen irked by the king's increasingly foolhardy attempts to invade Russia.

Following Gustave III's death (and the short-lived reign of his son, the unfortunately titled Gustave Adolf IV) Finland was ceded to Russia and became an autonomous grand duchy. Despite being, to all intents and purposes, part of the Russian Empire, Finland was able to instil its own constitution and relax some of the stringent controls that Gustave and Gustave Adolf had implemented (actually Gustave Adolf didn't do much, I just wanted to write his name again as I rather childishly think its funny).

Amongst the reforms was a repeal on the prohibition of the production of spirits and liqueurs. This led to a veritable explosion in home brewing in Finland throughout the early- to mid-ninteenth century and it is from this period that lakka was first developed. Once the shackles were off however, the Finns went a bit crazy on the home brewing front and, ever concerned about the effects of alcohol on the population, the government again banned home distilling in 1864, imposing strict licensing regulations. These restrictions decreed that spirits, the popularity of which had risen dramatically throughout the ninteenth century, could only be produced by licensed chemists. In 1872 two young scientists,

Hugo Lignell and August Piispanen, bought a run-down chemical dispensary in the town of Kuopio which stood on the site of King Gustave III's original royal distillery. Lignell and Piispanen's intention was the commercial production of traditional artisanal drinks such as Mesimarja (distilled Arctic bramble fire water) and lakka.

At the turn of the twentieth century a wave of Christian revivalism spread across Northern Europe which contributed greatly to the growing temperance movement. This led to Finland adopting what is known as the 'Gothenburg System' of alcohol control. The Gothenburg System is basically a state monopoly of the distribution of alcohol at the point of consumption i.e. the government owns all the pubs and therefore sets the prices.

Not content with controlling the who, what, where and when of Finnish drinking culture, following the Finnish Civil war in 1918, the government introduced blanket prohibition. Understandably, this severely affected Lignell and Piispanen's business. However they were able to survive by a peculiar loophole in the regulations. One legitimate way to purchase alcohol was via medical prescription and this led to a lucrative sideline for the medical profession through taking bribes for writing bogus scripts for patients. Far from stifling and ultimately eliminating the drinking culture, prohibition merely drove it underground with drinking taking on the form of a symbolic protest by the working classes against the state and the bourgeoisie. Subsequently prohibition, rather than quelling the social unrest caused by excessive alcohol consumption (a spurious claim made by temperance movements concerned with preserving 'national vitality') it actually had the opposite effect of inflaming and provoking the lower classes.

By 1932 the Finish state had realised the error of its ways; it called a referendum on the prohibition question and was forced to lift the ban. Somewhat reluctant to give the people what they wanted, however, Finland reverted to a hybridised version of the Gothenburg System and set up a state-owned company called ALKO to control all aspects of alcohol consumption. Between 1940–70, draconian restrictions existed in Finland that made licensing laws in the UK seem positively libertarian in comparison. These restrictions have gradually relaxed over the last forty years but it is still illegal to drink spirits until the age of 21 and illegal to produce or import spirits of a strength greater than 22 per cent ABV.

Lignell and Piispanen, along with Lapponia, are the principle producers of spirits and liqueurs in Finland, with the former specialising in 'lost' recipes from the ninteenth century such as lakka and fortified cloudberry wine.

TASTING NOTES: Lakka has as its primary flavouring the indigenous cloudberry. A cross between a wild raspberry and a hedgerow blackberry, cloudberries only grow in the desolate marshlands of Finland and Lapland. Lakka is produced by hand-picking these small yellow berries when in season and soaking them in a neutral alcohol base (low grade vodka is also used by some companies) for up to six months in oak barrels. Additional natural sweeteners such as honey and cinnamon are also added before further aging prior to bottling. The result is a rich, golden yellow syrupy liqueur with warming bitter sweet balances.

GOOD FOR: Staving off those suicidal urges during the short days of almost perpetual gloom of the Finnish winter.

COCKTAIL RECIPES

Cloudberry Dreams

4cl lakka
2.5cl akvavit
lemonade
ice cubes
twist of lime juice

Stir lakka and akvavit with ice in a tall glass, top up with lemonade and add a twist of lime juice.

Supersonic Gin and Tonic

2.5cl lakka
2.5cl Plymouth Gin
5cl tonic
ice cubes
slice of lemon

Mix the ingredients together and stir. Float the slice of lemon on the top.

FRANCE

Bénédictine

DESCRIPTION: Originally made in the sixteenth century by Benedictine monks as a herbal tonic and revived by Alexandre Legrand in 1863.

BACKGROUND: The story of Bénédictine begins in 1510 with the arrival at the Benedictine Abbey in Fécamp, Normandy, of a young Venetian monk, Dom Bernardo Vincelli. A skilled alchemist, Vincelli set about producing health elixirs by combining local herbs and different spices in cordials. News of the medicinal wonders of these creations spread to the court of François I, a man much enamoured with the latest renaissance trends. François visited Fécamp and declared: 'On my word as a gentleman! I have tasted nothing better' after sampling the monks' cordial. The king subsequently bestowed royal privilege and patronage upon the abbey.

For the next 150 years the monks continued to refine and develop their recipes in peaceful contemplation but suffered a similar fate to the Carthusian brothers of Voiron (*see* **Chartruse**). In 1791, due to the royal privileges bestowed upon them, the monks' abbey was one of the first seized and ransacked during the post-revolution purges. Having abolished the church's taxation rights, the new regime declared that all church property and land belonged to the nation and so appropriated what they could to be sold at public auction. The official in charge of selling off the monks' land and possessions was Prosper-Elie Covillard, fiscal prosecutor for the Fécamp region. Covillard came into possession of some of Bernando Vincelli's original manuscripts which he decided to keep for reasons unknown.

Sixty years passed with the manuscripts gathering dust in the attic until a descendent of Covillard, a local wine merchant named Alexandre Legrand, stumbled across them. Intrigued, Legrand enlisted the help of a local scholar and chemist to decipher the scripts and brewing formulas resulting, more or less, in the drink known today as Bénédictine.

The drink became an overnight sensation in France with some 28,000 bottles sold in the first year of production. Legrand registered the trademark in 1864 and embarked upon a revolutionary marketing campaign by commissioning artists to create beautiful art nouveau posters and press adverts, a promotional tactic that was soon adopted by other leading drinks manufacturers.

Legrand's principal passions were the fine arts and the success of his business enabled him to indulge this through his patronage of young and struggling artists whilst acquiring a significant private collection of his own. By 1882 demand for Bénédictine was far outstripping supply and Legrand (whom had by now changed his name to Le Grande, literally, Alexander the Great), embarked upon his most ambitious project to date.

The company was in dire need of new premises and so Legrand hit upon the idea of combining business with pleasure by building his new distillery inside an enormous palace which could also house his burgeoning collection of fourteenth and fifteenth-century classical and religious art. Legrand's first Palais de la Bénédictine opened in 1888 but was destroyed by a fire four years later. Taking the setback squarely on the chin, Legrand immediately set about rebuilding a larger and grander replacement, this time in an ostentatious faux gothic/romanesque style. Sadly, Legrand died before it was completed in 1900, however, it remains as a working distillery and art museum, a popular tourist attraction and a fitting monument to the flamboyance of the man who rescued Bénédictine from obscurity.

TASTING NOTES: Lacking the mesmeric colour and fountain of flavours of France's other great herbal elixir Chartreuse, Bénédictine is best used in cocktails or in the classic B and B (see below). Drunk neat, the initial sweet hints of cinnamon quickly subside into a bitter tang of gentian leaving a lingering after taste that is reminiscent of milk of magnesia.

GOOD FOR: Heartburn and stomach ulcers ... no, sorry, that's milk of magnesia. Bénédictine is very popular with tin miners in China who take flasks of it underground to counteract rheumatoid arthritis. The Bénédictine website contains several mouth-watering recipes for using Bénédictine in South East Asian cuisine as it lends itself especially well when added to fruit sauces and marinades for seafood.

TRIVIA: Every bottle of Bénédictine has the initials D.O.M. stamped on the label which, according to common ignorance, is taken to stand for Dominican Order of Monks. In truth, the initials form an acronym of the Latin phrase *Deo Optimo*

Maximo ('For our best, greatest God'), an inscription that appears above the doorways of many Renaissance era churches in Italy and reflects Alexandre Legrand's interest in Christian art and iconography.

Bénédictine are extremely guarded and precious about protecting their intellectual property rights. So much so that a room in Le Palais de la Bénédictine known as *Salle des Contrefaçons* (Hall of Counterfeits) is devoted to displaying a collection of imitation Bénédictine from around the world. The company embarked upon a long and protracted legal battle with the monks of the Santo Domingo de Silos Abbey in Northern Spain who produce a liqueur similar in taste to Bénédictine. However, Bénédictine lost out to the Spanish monks, who were able to demonstrate via manuscripts from their library, that they had in fact been producing their liqueur for several centuries longer than the abbey at Fécamp. The Santo Domingo de Silos monks reached international fame when their CD of Gregorian chants (imaginatively titled *Chant*) reached number 3 in the Billboard Top 200 and sold millions of copies around the world. Overall, they must be feeling pretty pleased with themselves.

The Burnley Miners Social Club is the world's hub of Bénédictine drinking with more bottles consumed per annum on the premises than any other establishment across the globe. The tradition of drinking Bénédictine at the club dates back to the First World War. Many miners were drafted into the Lancashire regiments to dig networks of tunnels between and beneath the trenches at the front. When a miner was killed in action a bottle of Bénédictine was sent back from France to the club and a solemn toast made in his honour.

B and B

In the decadent days of 1930s Paris, the chic drink in the salons and bordellos was the B and B: Bénédictine mixed with brandy and bitters. Aware of the popularity of the drink, Bénédictine started to produce a ready-mixed blend which is readily available in supermarkets to this day. However, Bénédictine use fairly low grade cognac in their blend and so as an elegant alternative try the following easy do-it-yourself mix.

The ratio of Bénédictine to brandy is a subject of some debate amongst mixologists. Traditionally the blend should be 50/50 but in the 1950s, New York cocktail bars began mixing B and Bs with cream into a long drink and using a 2/1 ratio in favour of Bénédictine. It's a matter of personal taste and one worth experimenting with until you find a blend that suits. I also recommended using reasonably expensive aged cognac (either VS or VSOP), if you are going to make a B and B it is worth doing it properly.

2cl Remy Martin VS or VSOP
2cl Bénédictine

Take a brandy snifter and measure out the Bénédictine and then gently float the measure of cognac by pouring over the back of a teaspoon. DO NOT STIR!

For the cream B and B, mix two parts Bénédictine with one part brandy of your choice (it would be sacrilegious to use an expensive cognac in this instance), blend in the cream and serve over ice.

Widow's Kiss

Created to 'marry' France's premier herbal liqueurs in 1895 by Parisian restaurateur Francois Le Colet.

2cl calvados
1cl Chartreuse (preferably yellow, but green can be substituted for an extra kick)
1cl Bénédictine
1 dash Angostura Bitters

Stir with ice in a cocktail shaker. Strain into a cocktail glass.

Chambord

DESCRIPTION: Black raspberry liqueur traditionally made in the Loire Valley.

BACKGROUND: Chambord is believed to have been created in honour of King Louis XIV of France during a stay at Château de Chambord in 1685. The longest-reigning European monarch in history (seventy-two years, three months, eighteen days) was rather partial to drinking cognac mixed with pressed fruits and so a local alchemist was employed to produce a concoction to be presented to the king at a royal banquet. Nestling in the Loire Valley, Château de Chambord was built by François I ostensibly as a holiday home close to the rural retreat of his mistress the Comtesse de Thoury. An elaborate castle/palace, Château de Chambord took over thirty years to build and was still incomplete when Francois died in 1547. The Château was left to fall into disrepair by successive kings, until Louis XVI decided to renovate the building in 1639 to use as a hunting lodge. The locals were obviously thrilled by the return of royal patronage and hence the creation of Chambord as a symbol of their appreciation.

The principle selling point of the drink is the use of wild black raspberries which are particular to the Loire Valley. These raspberries are soaked whole in a neutral spirit for several weeks along with local blackberries to create a rich infusion. This spirit infusion is then pressed and blended with oak aged cognac, red currents, cinnamon and honey to produce the liqueur before under going a second period of aging prior to bottling.

TASTING NOTES: The black raspberry aroma is very strong and suggests one is about to taste something truly remarkable. Sadly Chambord doesn't quite live up to this promise; the tartness of the *framboises noires* leaves a tang on the palette which is faintly reminiscent of children's cough medicine, not necessarily a bad thing to some tastes but for all the drink's hubris (Chambord is often referred to as Chambord Royale) and fancy bottle, it doesn't quite deliver the goods. It is quite mild though for a fruit based liqueur with an ABV of 16.5 per cent.

GOOD FOR: Excellent in cocktails, but then again most fruit liqueurs come into their own when mixed with other drinks so this is no great surprise. Chambord adds a lovely boozy kick to chocolate fondue or melted chocolate used for covering strawberries or cherries.

TRIVIA: Chambord has a distinctive round bottle adorned with gold plastic lettering and an elaborate crown crest on the top. The design is based upon the *globus cruciger*, a traditional symbol of Christian authority which is taken to signify Christ's dominion over the world. Although it looks very flashy, the plastic lettering is actually quite cheap and shoddy, although it may appeal to people with a taste for kitsch.

Academics have long debated who actually designed the Château de Chambord. The renaissance architect Philibert Delorme is credited with the initial designs but there is a theory that several of the elaborate staircases may have been created by Leonardo da Vinci.

French Kiss

Also known as Sex on the Pool Table, this makes an excellent party punch if the quantities are increased in equal parts.

2cl Midori melon liqueur
2cl Archers peach schnapps
2cl triple sec
2cl Chambord
2cl grapefruit juice

Mix well in a cocktail shaker and pour over crushed ice.

Gay Paris

1cl Chambord
1cl strawberry schnapps
2cl Amarreto
4cl milk

Stir in the measures and serve in a tall glass, milk should be chilled.

Chartreuse

DESCRIPTION: Wine-based herb and plant extract liqueur that has been made by monks according to an ancient manuscript for over 400 years.

BACKGROUND: In 1605, a prominent artillery marshal in the court of King Henry IV, Francois Annibal d'Estrees, presented the Carthusian monks ofVoiron with an alchemical manuscript that contained a recipe for an 'elixir of long life'. This manuscript contained an elaborate formula of over 130 different ingredients which, when combined with distilled wine, came to be known as 'Elixir Végétal de la Grande Chartreuse'. Formed by St Bruno in the eleventh century, the order of the Carthusians dedicate themselves to an eremitical way of life consisting of silent and solitary contemplation, scholarship, prayer, the wearing of skin-shredding goat hair shirts and, thanks largely to d'Estrees, the production and distillation of mind-bending liqueurs.

The eremitical life dictates that nothing, if anything at all, should be done in a hurry or without serious contemplation and so it is no surprise it took the monks of Chartreuse over 100 years to perfect their medicinal elixir. In 1737, Brother Gerome Maubec is credited with modifying the recipe and process to produce the basis of the drink we know today as Chatreuse. The drink became extremely popular, much to the bewilderment of the monks who found themselves somewhat pressed to keep up with demand. By 1764 the monks had expanded the distilleries within the abbey walls and produced a refined version of the elixir known as Green Chartreuse. However, the monks fell foul of the anti-clerical movement during the French Revolution and were expelled from their monastery and as result production of the drink ceased for nearly fifty years.

By 1838 relations between the Catholic Church and the state had thawed sufficiently to allow the monks to return to their monastery and resume their distilling. In celebration of their return, the order produced a new variety flavoured with saffron and lighter in alcohol known as Yellow Chartreuse. The reputation and popularity of Chartreuse continued to grow but sadly the monks again fell foul of state intervention when a change in the law regulating the production of alcohol saw them expelled in 1903 and their premises and assets confiscated by the government.

Undeterred by their treatment at the hands of the authorities, the monks simply wandered over the Pyrenees and settled in Tarragona, Spain. Armed with their now-sacred manuscript and hundreds of years of experience the Carthusian brothers continued living pretty much as they had always done: not speaking very much, wearing uncomfortable clothing and producing magical alcoholic beverages.

Meanwhile, mindful of the commercial potential of Chartreuse, the government sold the monastery's assets to a local corporation in Voiron who started producing a counterfeit version of the drink. This version of the drink did not have the benefit of the monks' mystical recipe and proved unpopular with the public. By 1927 the corporation was on the verge of bankruptcy and an enterprising group of Voiron residents bought up all of the shares of the company and sent them as a gift to the monks in Tarragona along with a plea for them to return. The monks were delighted to go back to the site where 800 years earlier St Bruno and six of his followers had first set up shop and took advantage of a peculiar legal loophole: although they were officially still banned from the area and had had their citizenship revoked, they effectively owned the Chartreuse company lock, stock and barrel.

This triumphant return was sadly short-lived. In 1935 disaster struck when a freak mudslide in the Voiron valley virtually destroyed the distillery. Heedful of their previous harsh treatment of the brothers, the French government detailed the army to salvage what they could from the wreckage and build them a new distillery which still survives to the present day.

TASTING NOTES: Chartreuse Green is the most popular variety and as with all herb-based liqueurs it benefits from being served well chilled over ice. A flurry of sweet aniseed gives way to God knows what (and in this case if anybody knows, then God surely does) followed by bitter undercurrents of minty hyssop. The overall 'hit'is quite beguiling and easy to see why the drink is afforded such worldwide devotion.

Chartreuse Yellow is milder and sweeter and can be served as a long drink with ice and two parts tonic. To commemorate the 400th anniversary of the drink, Chartreuse produced an approximation of Brother Gerome Maubec's original 'Elixir Végétal de la Grande Chartreuse' in a limited edition bottle of 10cl. Weighing in at an impressive 71 per cent ABV and packaged in a sunlight-proof wooden box, this elixir is firewater of the highest order. It is 'taken' by drizzling four or five drops (a pipette is recommended) over a sugar cube and dissolving into a little touch of warm water. Not a tipple for the faint-hearted but after taking the elixir a few moments of silent contemplation should be dutifully observed in honour of the Carthusian brothers and their trials through the ages.

GOOD FOR: Those awkward moments when pious, god-fearing relatives pay a visit and pass snide comment on the 'demon drink'.

TRIVIA: The monks take the protection of their recipe extremely seriously. One monk is in sole possession of the manuscript and he in turn imparts one third of the ingredients to two other designated 'producers'. Before a monk dies, he nominates a replacement to be taught his third of the recipe.

Chartreuse has enjoyed a cult following amongst writers and artists and as a result literature and films are littered with various references to the drink. Nick Carraway enjoys a glass of Chartreuse on the night he first meets his elusive eponymous anti-hero in F. Scott-Fitzgerald's *The Great Gatsby*. In *Brideshead Revisited* by Evelyn Waugh, Anthony Blanche and Charles Ryder drink Chartreuse after dinner with Anthony observing that their *digestif* is 'Real G-g-green Chartreuse, made before the expulsion of the monks. There are five distinct tastes as it trickles over the tongue. It is like swallowing a sp-spectrum.'

Le Classique

Grande Chartreuse

5cl Green Chartreuse
50cl gin
splash of orange bitters
splash of dry vermouth

Combine ingredients in an ostentatiously tall glass (for that added touch wet the rim of the glass in lemon or lime juice and dip in sugar) and sprinkle with a little finely chopped mint.

Backdraft

1.5cl Green Chartreuse
1.5cl black sambuca
3cl Green Chartreuse
4 or 5 pinches cinnamon powder

Created by master mixologist Alex Schultz, this cocktail is more than a little tricky to pull off and arguably downright dangerous. Take a shot glass, place it on a glass saucer and add the small measure of Chartreuse and a layer of black sambuca. Take a separate highball glass, add the large measure of Chartreuse and set fire to it. While the large glass is flaming, pour it over the shot glass for that thrill of trying to put out a bonfire with a can of petrol effect. If you haven't received third degree burns by this point, sprinkle the cinnamon powder on to the flames to make it spit and sparkle. Quickly hold the empty highball glass over the flames to capture the alcohol vapour. After roughly ten seconds (assuming you are relatively unscathed), trap the vapour with a coaster and invite somebody to down the shot, inhale the vapour and slurp up anything left in the saucer. This is clearly a cocktail which appeals primarily to pyromaniacs and anybody preparing it, or drinking it for that matter, does so at their own risk.

Crème de Violette

DESCRIPTION: Brandy or neutral-based liqueur flavoured with Alpine violet petals, much sought after by cocktail aficionados.

BACKGROUND: Crème de violette started life as a sweet cordial popular in French coffee houses in the early to mid nineteenth century. By the 1860s, the popularity of fruit brandies and herbal liqueurs led to the production of a crème de violette blended with either cheap brandy or neutral base alcohol which was often drunk as an accompaniment to dessert in Parisian restaurants.

Perhaps because of its rich natural colouring and deep flowery bouquet, crème de violette never quite reached the heights of public consciousness afforded to France's other great flagship spirits and liqueurs; almost as if a mild, sweet and fragrant drink made ostensibly from wild flowers lacked the eye watering machismo of Bénédictine or the arty underclass chic of Absinthe. Whatever the reason, large scale industrial production of crème de violette never took off and the drink slipped gradually into obscurity.

By the second decade of the twentieth century, the era of the great aviators had begun. Many a wealthy work-shy fop jumped on the bandwagon and planned increasingly ludicrous ventures to be 'the first' to fly from point A to point B (and more often than not, ending up landing ignominiously at point C). To commemorate these largely fruitless endeavours, barman Hugo Ensslin of the Hotel Wallick in New York created the Aviation cocktail (see recipe below). The original Aviation, according to Ensslin's 1916 classic book *Recipes for Mixed Drinks*, required crème de violette as its secret ingredient in order to produce a beautiful sky blue hue to the concoction. One could sip an Aviation and marvel at man's quest to conquer the mysteries of flying into the wild (sky) blue yonder. Or at least I think that was the idea.

However, due to the scarcity of crème de violette and the onset of prohibition in 1920, the popularity of the Aviation proved short-lived. By 1930, the legendary Harry Craddock – head barman at the American Bar in the Savoy Hotel, London – had tired of the unavailability of crème de violette and omitted it from the Aviation recipe in the first edition of his *Savoy Cocktail Book,* preferring to substitute an extra shot of gin.

Crème de violette continued to recede slowly into anonymity, a mere footnote in the history of mixed drinks, until salvation of sorts arrived in the form of Eric Seeds, a drinks importer and amateur cocktail historian. Seeds has been described by the American drinks writer Camper English as the 'Indiana Jones of lost spirits' due to his dedication to tracking down and reviving long-forgotten spirit brands and liqueurs. In 2007, Seeds persuaded the Austrian drinks distillery Purkhart to produce a 'new' crème de violette using a maceration of wild Alpine Queen Charlotte and March violets distilled in 'Weinbrand' (a white grape distillate used in German dessert wines). The result is the Rothman and Winter Crème de Violette which Seeds sells through his online rare drinks emporium Haus Alpenz, much to the delight of cocktail bloggers and drinks 'trainspotters' the world over.

TASTING NOTES: Rothman and Winter Crème de Violette, the most easily available incarnation of this generic liqueur, is the one to go for if buying on the internet. No doubt there are better, more flowery varieties available in obscure regions of France but the R&W remains a safe bet. The first hurdle to clear when opening a bottle of R&W is the bouquet, which is not quite the fresh burst of the hills being alive with the smell of freshly picked violets that one might have hoped for; no cute von Trapp kids gurgling, no Julie Andrews. On the contrary, it is more reminiscent of searching desperately through the medicine cabinet to try and find something to alleviate a monstrous hangover. The smell of aging aspirin aside (easily dissipated by allowing the bottle to breathe for twenty minutes), this is actually a very fine and versatile drink. Poured into shots as an aperitif or used in a multitude of highbrow cocktails – the flowery, sweet and soapy hit is not unlike children's sweets such as the classic Pez or 1950s Violet Candies in the US.

GOOD FOR: Other than to use in a brace of classic cocktails, crème de violette is much sought-after by makers of fine, bespoke chocolates and sweet meats.

TRIVIA: The scarcity of crème de violette was used as a key component in an episode of 1960s television programme *The Avengers*. On the hunt for a mysterious Eastern European dissident with an unquenchable thirst for cigars, model aeroplanes and (you guessed it!) crème de violette, urbane spy John Steed bribes a half-witted Russian stooge with a bottle of the hard-to-find liqueur.

The Aviation

A much messed-about-with cocktail with numerous different versions jockeying for position (some use Crème Yvette, which imparts a completely different tone to the combination of flavours). This, as far as I can tell, is Hugo Ensslin's original Aviation recipe from the height of the cocktail age:

2.5cl gin (preferably Plymouth or London)
1cl Maraschino
1cl fresh lemon juice
1cl crème de violette
a slice of flamed lemon peel

Pour the ingredients into a shaker filled with crushed ice, strain and serve garnished with lemon peel slices.

The Blue Moon

It must be something to do with the obscurity of crème de violette but there are also numerous different versions of this other 'classic', some substituting Blue Curaçao to provide the colouring which is just plain wrong. The version below has a bit of a kick to it courtesy of the added shot of tequila.

2.5cl gin
1cl crème de violette
1cl tequila
a twist of lemon juice

Mix in a shaker and pour over crushed ice.

La Fée Absinthe

DESCRIPTION: Most popular brand of French absinthe throughout the ninteenth century until it was banned in 1915. La Fée was the first Absinthe to be produced through traditional methods when the prohibition of absinthe in France was lifted.

BACKGROUND: Absinthe can be traced to a patented medicine conceived as an 'elixir of life' created from wormwood distillate by Dr. Pierre Ordinaire, a French medic working in Switzerland in the 1790s. Two local businessmen, Henri Louis Pernod and Daniel Henri Dubied, acquired the recipe and set up production in Couvet in 1797, later moving to larger premises in the town of Pontarlier, France, in 1805.

The classic absinthe recipe requires macerating wormwood, fennel, melissa and anise in a neutral wine-based alcohol before distilling in a copper still to produce a transparent liquid. The colouring is added with of hyssop and petit wormwood which is distilled and blended separately before mixing with the base. The olive green tint that the additional herbs impart and its extraordinarily high alcohol content (68 per cent ABV) led to the drink gaining the nickname '*La Fée Verte*' (the Green Fairy).

Pernod and Dubied's factory quickly established Pontarlier as the centre of absinthe production in the nineteenth century with at one time over twenty different companies producing the drink in the town. Production of Pernod Fils alone rose from a modest 16 litres a day to over 30,000. The rise of absinthe as a social phenomenon and subsequent backlash presents something of a conundrum to historians. Favorite tipple of writers and poets, absinthe was immortalised in famous paintings by the likes of Degas, Manet and van Gogh. However, all of these props from figures of the '*Belle Epoque*' could not by themselves have accounted to the spectacular growth in absinthe consumption.

In the 1850s English botanists brought home grape vine samples from North America. These samples carried an unwanted stowaway in the form of Phylloxera, a microscopic aphid-like insect that has a ravenous appetite for vine roots and leaves. The sudden inexplicable deterioration of grapevines first surfaced in the southern Rhône region but quickly spread across the continent. France was the most severely affected with annual production of wine falling from 85 million litres to 22 million litres in under fifteen years. The effect on the industry was catastrophic and sowed a simmering discontent that eventually exploded in the Champagne riots of 1910 and 1911.

With over two thirds of French vineyards destroyed by the Phylloxera epidemic, wine was in increasingly short supply and sold at hugely inflated prices. Absinthe was the main beneficiary as it was cheaper and more easily available. It was also nearly six times as strong as an average red table wine and consequently led to a huge increase in alcohol related illness and death.

At the turn of the twentieth century the temperance movement was gathering momentum across Europe and America and attracting the support of leading politicians keen to blame societal ills on the demon drink. On the afternoon of 28 August 1905, Swiss farm labourer Jean Lanfray returned home after a lunchtime drinking binge and shot his wife and two young daughters. Lanfray's father escaped and testified that his son had flown into a drunken rage because his wife had refused to polish his boots. It was reported that Lanfray had been drinking absinthe and this was seized upon by supporters of the temperance movement as evidence in their bid to get the drink banned. In actuality, Lanfray had drunk only one large measure of absinthe but had polished off seven glasses of wine, six of cognac, two menthol liqueurs and one large brandy with his coffee, so it is unlikely that the absinthe was the sole cause of his ire. Nonetheless, the Lanfray case sparked a moral panic across Europe, resulting in Belgium, Sweden and Switzerland banning the drink within two years of the murders.

The French Government initially resisted the clamour for prohibitive measures, largely on the grounds that the French were consuming an astonishing 36 million litres of the drink per annum. The ensuing riots and public unrest in the wine growing regions, coupled with the rash of cheap, unregulated and downright dangerous absinthe imitations flooding the market, caused an abrupt u-turn in 1915 when absinthe was finally outlawed. Pernod Fils moved its distillery to Tarragona, Spain where production continued on a smaller scale until the 1960s. Gradually though, other drinks filled the chasm left by absinthe's demise with Pernod's own liqueur, d'anise, gaining popularity despite possessing only a passing relationship to the original drink. Absinthe never regained its popularity and lived on only in parts of central and eastern Europe, where any faintly aniseed flavoured, high strength liqueur could be passed off as absinthe.

The myths and legends of absinthe persisted throughout the twentieth century but the ban remained in place until 1998. George Rowley, a British drinks importer, got together with micro-biologist and absinthe scholar Marie-Claude Delahaye to recreate a traditional classic absinthe brand La Fée. Rowley successfully lobbied the UK Government and as a result absinthe is available again across the EU. With a nice nod to authenticity and history, La Fée is being produced in the suburbs of Pontarlier once more.

TASTING NOTES: Pernod's '68' Absinthe, re-launched after the ban was lifted is a big disappointment and had many an absinthe enthusiast in a rage about the cynical use of the Pernod name. The main problem stems from an over-reliance of anise and the use of artificial colourings. The absence of the fragrant alpine herbs such as hyssop also severely affect the bouquet of the 'new' Pernod, leaving the feeling that you are drinking a rather jumped-up cousin of Pernod's bog standard pastis. Pernod-Ricard's suggestion that it is 'derived' from the original recipe is not to be taken at face value.

La Fée Green has more authentic claims on account of being the first produced in Pontarlier after the ban was lifted. The nose has a much more floral tone to it and when mixed with water the lovely louche effect of absinthe comes into play. When sweetened with sugar, the final after notes are far milder on the star anise than many higher-priced absinthes and the drink leaves a pleasant chalky residue. .

GOOD FOR: There is a lot of nonsense attached to absinthe; exaggerated claims about its hallucinogenic, quasi-mystical properties abound, but beyond all that the fact remains that few drinks in world have such a rich historical and cultural cachet. High class silversmiths in Paris spent decades producing intricate designs to try and perfect the perfect absinthe spoon for dissolving sugar. There is no other drink that accessorises in the same way. The art and poetry the drink inspired comprises a highly impressive portfolio of ninteenth-century European culture. In short, absinthe is not just good, it is truly great.

Absinthe is best taken by dissolving in a lump of sugar with lukewarm water until the mixture becomes milky and then stirring gently, leaving to settle and slowly drinking down in one, holding a little residue on the palette. I can guarantee that twenty minutes later the world will seem a better place (unless, of course, you are a Swiss farm worker with dirty boots).

TRIVIA: Volunteers in the French Foreign Legion received a bottle of absinthe in their rations as a preventative antidote to malaria and other tropical diseases in the 1840s and 1850s.

Also of peculiar note is the French government's preposterous ideas for compensating absinthe producers after the ban came into effect. One scheme involved the distilleries who had huge unsellable stock piles of the drink selling their product to the French Ministry of Defence to be redistilled, filtered and used in weapons development during the First World War as low-grade gunpowder for shells.

GERMANY

Goldwasser

DESCRIPTION: Amber-coloured herbal liqueur from the sixteenth century that contains flecks of 18–22 carat gold.

BACKGROUND: Alchemy was all the rage in sixteenth-century Europe and the ancient German city of Danzig caught the zeitgeist with the introduction of Goldwasser in 1598. The two main pursuits of alchemy were largely centred on fruitless attempts to turn lead (or just about any other substance) into gold and the creation of panaceas – magical health potions to cure illness and promote eternal life. Goldwasser bridges these twin endeavours by being an elixir of life that contains gold as a constituent part.

The man credited with creating Goldwasser was a Dutch-born alchemist by the name of Ambrose Vermollen. Vermollen was a member of the Mennonite Christian sect, an offshoot of the Anabaptist movement. Mennonites were followers of the writings of a radical Dutch catholic priest Menno Simons, who rejected traditional catholic practices such as infant baptism and the concept of transubstantiation. Not for the first time in history, the Roman Catholic Church hierarchy took quite an exception to Menno Simons and his followers and set about a relentless program of purges involving judicious use of torture and execution on the grounds of heresy. As a result, the sect soon became dispersed and exiled across Europe before eventually developing into other Anabaptist sects such as the Amish.

Vermollen is believed to have been granted citizenship of Danzig towards the end of the sixteenth century and created Danziger Goldwasser (Gold Water of Danzig) as a gift to the city for providing him with sanctuary from the Inquisition. Vermollen started a small distillery, which he called Der Lachs on account of the metal sculpture of a salmon that hung above the doorway (houses in Danzig were not distinguished by numbers but by animal symbols). Goldwasser became something of a sensation, with the fame of the golden drink spreading across Europe. Louis XIV was an early champion of Goldwasser, as was Peter the Great of Russia who became enamoured with the drink after visiting Danzig on one of his many European tours.

Goldwasser continued to be produced in Danzig up until the First World War when the city was separated from Germany by the Polish Corridor. The Der Lachs company moved production to Berlin in 1922 and after Danzig was incorporated into Poland after the Second World War (renamed Gdańsk), the Berlin factory became the sole producer of Goldwasser.

TASTING NOTES: Goldwasser is comprised of a medley of different roots, herbs and spices including cardamom, coriander, cinnamon, lavender, cloves, juniper and thyme. The flecks of gold provide an attractive glitter effect when holding a glass up to sunlight and giving the mixture a gentle swirl but, contrary to the manufacturer's claims, they impart little flavour or benefit other than the purely cosmetic. Der Lachs Danziger, being the original and best (there are several inferior imitations claiming to be Danzig Gold Water and also cheap rival drink Goldschläger) has a syrupy consistency. The initial herbal hit of cinnamon fools you into thinking the drink may be a little too sweet for some tastes but actually there are pleasant secondary tones of thyme and a slightly gin-like fragrance that balances the sweetness out.

GOOD FOR: A dessert soufflé created by Marie-Antoine Carême, the self styled 'King of Chefs' and creator of haute cuisine, for Baron James Mayer de Rothschild and Baroness Betty de Rothschild in the 1820s. The Baron was a notable French banker and diplomat. Marie-Antoine Carême's original recipe contained Goldwasser but several modern variations have replaced it with other liqueurs and cherry brandies.

TRIVIA: The site of Vermollen's original distillery is now occupied by one of Poland's most famous restaurants: Pod Lososiem (The Salmon). The restaurant has a beautiful pseudo nineteenth-century art nouveau interior and specialises mainly in seafood. Culinary opinion is divided as to the validity of Pod Lososiem's lofty reputation with some critics pointing out that the owners are particularly pleased with their impressive list of clients: a wall of fame in the entrance shows you that George Bush, Margaret Thatcher, Pope John Paul II and Danzig-born Nobel Laureate Günter Grass have all eaten there. A cheaper alternative, but without the historical cache, is Gdańsk's riverside Goldwasser Restaurant which also contains a mini museum dedicated to the drink and sells all manner of Goldwasser-related merchandise.

Golden Fleece

2.5cl Danziger Goldwasser
5cl Yellow Chartreuse
ice cubes

Carefully measure out ingredients into cocktail shaker and stir, strain over ice cubes.

A variation of this cocktail called the Golden Slipper appears in the Savoy cocktail book but consists of one shot of Goldwasser, one shot of Yellow Chartreuse and is shaken with an egg yolk to make an emulsion. The shaking of the mixture nullifies the sparkle effect of the flecks of the gold, however.

49er

Created in honour of the California Gold Rush and a mainstay of San Francisco's cocktail circuit.

2.5cl white rum
2.5cl cognac
2.5cl Danziger Goldwasser
ice cubes
twist of lemon juice
1 cherry

Stir ingredients in a cocktail shaker, strain over ice, add twist of lemon juice and garnish with a cherry.

Jägermeister

DESCRIPTION: Sickly sweet herbal liqueur that represents a triumph of clever marketing and corporate sponsorship.

BACKGROUND: Walk into any student union bar in the UK and it won't be long before you hear the name Jägermeister. The 'get wrecked quick' drink of choice for students aged between eighteen and twenty-four does, however, have a more than murky past which even the most politically disinterested student would baulk at if they knew.

The story of Jägermeister, or rather the Jägermeister 'brand' begins in earnest in 1930s Germany in the town of Wolfenbüttel in lower Saxony. For several centuries Wolfenbüttel had held a reputation as a centre for arts, culture and enlightened thinking (one of Europe's first lending libraries was established in the town). It was here that in 1922 the NSDAP (Nazi Party) established their first constituency outside of Bavaria and over the following decade developed into a leading political force in the area. A region of wide open spaces, gentle hills and forests, Wolfenbüttel became one of the centres for the Nazi's '*Kraft Durch Freude*' ('Strength Through Joy') programme, a politically motivated tourist company/charity that gave ordinary German workers on low incomes the chance to indulge in suitably agrarian outdoor pursuits such as hunting and fishing while sporting tight leather shorts and guzzling vast quantities of beer. Several of the leading lights of the Nazi Party attended these shindigs, with Josef Göbbels noting in his diaries the tremendous fun that was had by all.

Wolfenbüttel was also the hometown of local businessman and conservative politician Curt Mast. Mast had inherited the Findel-Mast family business in 1917 but the economic crisis in Germany that ensued after the First World War had seen the company teeter on the brink of bankruptcy. A keen hunting enthusiast, Mast is believed to have met Herman Göring sometime in the early 1930s and, sharing a passion for hunting, the two men became firm friends. At this point, the historical veracity of what followed starts to get cloudy. Mast held the seat of deputy minister in the local parliament, representing the Deutsche Volkspartei group. On 1 May 1933, Mast left the DVP and joined the Nazi Party. The reasons behind Mast's sudden change of allegiance are a matter of considerable conjecture. Political instability on a local and national level could have forced Mast into joining the National Socialists, or maybe he was, as he claimed after the war, merely a businessman wishing to exploit powerful contacts. The latter is certainly true of his association with Göring.

In 1934, Göring's role as interior minister allowed him to push through a private hunting bill known as the *Reichsjagdgesetz* (Reich Hunting Laws). Alongside the usual Nazi obsessions with building hierarchies of power (the law created regional *Jägermeisters* or 'Master Hunters' to act as administrators) stood some actually very progressive reforms in the area of animal rights. Hunting with dogs on horseback was banned, the killing of vixens with cubs was also outlawed and strict licensing controls were brought in. Some historians have noted that Hitler and Göring's hunting regulations actually had little to do with concerns for animal welfare and were merely part of a concerted attack upon the German aristocracy. Hitler and Göring had a dream of giving each of the Jägermeisters their own private hunting grounds as a symbol of their position of privilege within the Reich. Curt Mast became a Jägermeister and organised hunting parties for leading Nazi dignitaries at the Reichsjägerhof, Göring's hunting lodge. Sensing an opportunity to rebuild his business interests on the back of his association with the new hunting fraternity, Mast rebranded the herbal liqueur that his company produced as the official drink of the hunt. Hence the distinctive label adorned

with an image of a stag and the green glass bottle (green is the traditional colour of the huntsman).

The popularity of Jägermeister increased markedly during the years leading up to the Second World War with newspaper *Braunschweiger Zeitung* noting in 1938 that 'Jägermeister is highly valued in all German districts and ships.' The drink also became very popular with leading members of the German military, so much so that during the war it was often referred to by the nickname 'Göring-Schnapps.'

At the end of the war, Mast was summoned to appear before the British military governor of Wolfenbüttel and called to account for his Nazi associations. Somehow Mast managed to convince the governor that he was never actually a fully-fledged member of the party and was not put on trial. Mast returned to politics a few years later as a member of parliament for the Christian Democratic Union. The popularity of Jägermeister dipped after the war but it continued to be produced in Wolfenbüttel until Curt Mast's death in 1970.

Control of the brand then fell into the hands of Curt Mast's nephew Günter. A keen sports fan, Günter set about building up the brand through shrewd sponsorship of his local football team Eintracht Braunschweig and by attaching the Jägermeister name to international motor racing events. More recently the brand has attempted to garner a more youthful demographic through the sponsorship of music events and festivals, most notably large tours undertaken by American heavy rock bands such as Slipknot and Mötley Crüe. The popularity of Jägermeister has rocketed in the last decade, especially in the US where sales have quadrupled in the last five years alone. All in all, the drink has come a long way from being enthusiastically guzzled at Herman Göring's hunting parties.

TASTING NOTES: Jägermeister shares several similar characteristics with other central European herbal liqueurs such as Unicum and Becherovka. All three claim to be produced by an elaborate blend of over fifty herbs, roots and spices. Whereas Unicum, although pretty fearsome stuff, has some appeal on the grounds of trying to decipher the medley of flavours, Jägermeister is actually not as complicated as the brand likes to claim. The general tones are of sweet liquorice and star anise with a slightly citrus finish.

GOOD FOR: Upsetting students by pointing out that they are drinking 'Göring-Schnapps' and that isn't really very cool at all.

TRIVIA: The Jägermeister bottle sports verses from a poem believed to be the work of nineteenth-century naturalist and writer Oskar von Riesenthal. Riesenthal wrote many books on ornithology, natural preservation and hunting and his homespun philosophy would have appealed to Hitler and Göring's agrarian aesthetics:

Das ist des Jägers Ehrenschild,
daß er beschützt und hegt sein Wild,
weidmännisch jagt, wie sich's gehört,
den Schöpfer im Geschöpfe ehrt.

It is the hunter's honour that he
Protects and preserves his game,
Hunts sportsmanlike, honours the
Creator in His creatures.

Widow Maker

2.5cl Jägermeister
2.5cl vodka
2.5cl Kahlua
splash or two of Grenadine

Blend ingredients with some gentle shaking and ice, strain into cocktail glass.

Raspberry Beret

2.5cl Jägermeister
2.5cl vodka
2.5cl tequilla
5cl raspberry juice
splash or two of Grenadine

Named after the song by Prince. Stir ingredients in a cocktail shaker and pour into a highball glass with ice.

GREECE

Mastichato Chios

DESCRIPTION: Brandy-based liqueur flavoured with aromatic resin from the *Pistacia Lentiscus* tree (mastic).

BACKGROUND: Mastichato Chios is a traditional homemade liqueur native to the Greek island of Chios. Its distinctive strong liquorice-like flavouring comes from soaking resin extracted from the mastic tree in base alcohol and then double distilling the mixture before filtering through mastic roots.

Mastic is cultivated by bleeding the bark of the tree by slicing into the trunk and principal branches and allowing its distinctive milky sap to run out into special containers. The liquid is then left in the sun to harden and form into lumps of translucent waxy resin. When chewed and mixed with saliva the resin forms into an off-white gum. As a result, mastic has been used in various forms for the production of chewing gum dating back to the Roman Empire.

The production and harvesting of mastic on Chios has been strictly administrated and controlled since medieval times by a co-operative of small villages on the southern peninsula of the island known as the Mastichochoria. Although the mastic tree grows in various parts of the Mediterranean, mastic is only produced on Chios. Since the mastic trade is a major pillar of the local economy, Chios is protected by the European Union under their Protected Designation of Origin system (the same system that protects champagne) thereby prohibiting any other country or region from 'weeping' their mastic trees to procure resin.

Protection of Chios mastic production dates back to the Ottoman Empire. Mastic was highly praised by the sultans, whose harems used it as breath freshener and in the creation of cosmetics. Subsequently, when Greece fell under Ottoman rule the island of Chios was left alone to more or less self-govern and subsequently became one of the most prosperous islands in the Aegean Sea.

Chios' privileges under Ottoman rule came to a spectacular and bloody end with the Chios Massacre. In March 1822, a year into the Greek revolt against Ottoman rule, a young Greek revolutionary, Lykourgos Logothetis, led a small invasion force from neighbouring Samos to Chios with the intention of agitating the local inhabitants and turning the island against the Sultan. After burning down a few of the island's mosques and attacking Turkish settlers, Logothetis called a meeting with the island's ruling elite to try to persuade Chios to join the revolt. Although there was some sympathy for the cause, the elders of the island decided that they had a good deal to lose in terms of prosperity and peace and very little to gain given that Chios is dangerously close to the Turkish coastline, and so politely declined, preferring if possible to stay neutral.

Unfortunately news of Logothetis' ransacking of the mosques had reached the Sultan and, enraged by what he unfairly perceived as treachery on the part of the islanders, he promptly dispatched the Turkish fleet to exact revenge. On Good Friday 1822, the fleet landed on Chios and began a three-week orgy of murder and destruction. Churches were razed to the ground, entire villages butchered and thousands of the islanders rounded up and starved or tortured to death. Estimates on the scale of the massacre range from between 25,000 to 60,000 islanders killed and up to 50,000 taken into slavery. Only 2,000 of the islanders survived, mostly by hiding in caves or via the Sultan's orders that the people of the Mastichochoria were to be saved in order to protect the production of mastic.

Mastichato Chios is drunk primarily as a *digestif* either with dessert or with Greek starters (*mezés*).

TASTING NOTES: Mastichato Chios has a pleasant smell with strong tones of liquorice. Although seemingly sweet and aniseed-like there are harsher tones reminiscent of strong peppermint.

GOOD FOR: As an accompaniment to the classic Greek starter of calamari, fried courgettes, grilled sardines and stuffed vine leaves. Also works well to flambé pan-fried lambs' kidneys for a devilled effect.

Head in the Clouds

2.5cl Mastichato
2.5cl Blue Curaçao
2.5cl Baileys Irish Cream

Stir the Mastichato together with the Curacao and then float the Baileys on the top by pouring over the back of a chilled teaspoon.

Hot Greek Martini

2.5cl Mastichato
2.5cl vodka
5cl tonic
star anise

Stir the Mastichato and vodka, top up with tonic and float a star anise on the top as a garnish.

HUNGARY

Unicum Zwack

DESCRIPTION: Herb-based liqueur made from a blend of over forty different herbs and spices, usually drunk ice cold as a *digestif* or mixed in cocktails.

BACKGROUND: When in 1790 Dr Jozsef Zwack, royal physician to the Habsburg dynasty, was summoned by the dying Holy Roman Emperor Joseph II, he could scarcely have anticipated the impact he was about to make on future events in Hungarian history. The emperor, bedridden and crippled with stomach cramps, pleaded with Dr Zwack to give him something to alleviate the pain. The good doctor produced a herbal remedy he had been working on, probably more out of desperation than anything else and, to his astonishment, the emperor is reputed to have sat bolt up right in bed and cried '*Das est ein unikum*!' ('This is unique!'). The legend of Unicum was born.

Fifty years passed before the drink was formally put into commercial production by the grandson of Dr Zwack (also named Jozsef) who founded J. Zwack and Co., Hungary's first and therefore oldest distillery. Jozsef Zwack oversaw the growth of the company which expanded rapidly throughout the ninteenth century to become one of the leading liquor producers in Central Europe and continued to monitor every aspect of the company up to his death in 1915 at the ripe old age of 95 (Jozsef put his good health and longevity down to his twice daily 'tot' of Unicum). The reins of the family business passed first to Jozsef's son Lajos and then to Lajos' sons Bela and Janos.

The Zwack brand continued to prosper up until the Second World War when the factory was destroyed in the siege of Budapest. In 1948, the occupying Russians nationalised the business and Janos Zwack and his son Peter fled the country with the 'secret' recipe (see below), taking refuge in the United States. Bela remained behind and provided the communists with a counterfeit Zwack for the rebuilt state-owned factory. After several months on Ellis Island, Janos and Peter were granted US citizenship – apocryphally said to have been on the strength of holding the secret recipe. During the 1956 Hungarian Uprising and its aftermath, Peter Zwack travelled across America raising funds for the 200,000 refuges of the conflict and spreading awareness of the plight of his fellow countrymen.

As the communist regime began to crumble in the late 1980s, a popular movement started in Hungary to bring Unicum back home from the US, where the original formula had been kept in a safe deposit box in a New York bank for nearly forty years. In 1989, Peter Zwack returned to Budapest and bought the company out of state ownership. A returning champion of the people, the new post-communist Hungarian government acknowledged Peter's folk hero status by appointing him the first ambassador to the United States in 1991.

TASTING NOTES: The secret of Unicum's 'secret' recipe lies in the exact blend of the herbs and spices. Some of the herbs are distilled, others macerated with the ratio of the liquor extracted from the dual method blended to a precise balance. The resulting liqueur is then aged in oak casks for over six months to give it a dark, amber colouring. Joszef Zwack claimed that he could tell if one of the ingredients had been left out of the process and designated 'tasters' are still employed by the company to detect the subtlest of variations. Beyond all of Unicum's colourful history and the specific attention to detail in production the question remains: does it actually taste any good? Sadly, the answer is a pretty resounding 'no'. Unicum has a slightly musky aroma, reminiscent of mildew and a bitter opening blast of battery acid is quickly replaced by a lingering rusting iron water-butt aftertaste.

GOOD FOR: Getting rid of unwanted or persistent guests at drinks parties. Bring out the Unicum and people have a strange knack of suddenly remembering they should be elsewhere.

TRIVIA: One of Unicum's prime selling points is the inimitable design of its bottle. The distinctive, cartoon bomb shape adorned by a paramilitary red cross is a reference to the 1956 Hungarian uprising. Legend has it that some enterprising students broke into the Zwack factory and commandeered empty Unicum bottles to make Molotov cocktails, which were subsequently used against the advancing Russian tanks during the siege of Budapest. Ironically, Peter Zwack narrowly escaped an assassination attempt in 1992 when his Budapest flat was fire-bombed. Zwack had been recalled from his seat in Washington after publicly criticising the Hungarian government and subsequently stripped of his Ambassador post. The arson attack was believed to have been the work of disgruntled communist sympathisers.

Long, Slow, Cabbage in the Dark

2.5cl Unicun
2.5cl sloe gin (or patxaran)
7.5cl tonic
dash of pomegranate juice

Mix in a tall glass with tonic water and a dash of pomegranate juice ('Long'), a shot of sloe gin ('Slow') and a large shot of Unicum ('Cabbage in The Dark').

INDIA

Feni

DESCRIPTION: Liqueur made from either cashew apples or coconut. The most popular brand is Big Boss.

BACKGROUND: Feni, (sometimes spelt Fenny) derives from the popular Indian tourist resort area of Goa. Feni is specific to Goa and the word is a generic term for homemade or home distilled alcohol made principally from either the collected sap of coconut trees or cashew apples. The cashew apple liqueur is more prevalent and the Goan authorities have lobbied the World Trade Organisation for a Geographical Indicator for this type of feni in order to protect its production and develop export markets.

The origins of the production of feni are unknown but it is likely that the drink developed sometime in the early sixteenth century with the arrival of Portuguese traders who set up a coastline colony and introduced the cashew tree from South

America. The cashew apple is a large, bulbous heart-shaped pseudo fruit that grows around the cashew kernels that are harvested for the popular cashew 'nut'.

The traditional location for making feni is on rocky hillside outcrops where the cashew trees grow in wild abundance. The cashew apples are macerated in a hand-carved stone basin called a *coimbi* with the initial juice allowed to run out into huge earthenware pots that are buried in the ground. The cashew pulp is then moulded into a cake-shaped disc and bound with a string mesh. A large boulder is rolled on top of the pulp cakes and left for the remaining clear juice to trickle out which is known as *neero*. The *neero* is believed to have medicinal qualities and is taken as a local Goan remedy to relieve constipation.

The collected juice is then distilled three times to produce three grades: *urrack*, *cazulo* and *feni*. The distillation process also traditionally occurs on the hillside where the fruits were macerated. The mixture is siphoned from its underground tank into a simple still consisting of a *bhann*, usually a covered copper boiling pot, which is connected via pipes to a smaller pot, and the *launni* to collect the distillate. A large fire is lit beneath the *bhann* to provide a furious heat to kickstart the distillation process but as time progresses and the distillate forms in the *launni*, the temperature is carefully controlled by ladling on cold water and reducing the heat. This is a highly precarious process, lasting from eight to ten hours, and is usually undertaken by skilled groups of men who make up these hillside distilling parties known as *bhattis*.

The first distillation of the *bhatti* produces *urrack*, a milder variety that is usually drunk as a *digestif* after meals or mixed with fruit juices and soda. The second grade *cazulo* is stronger and also consumed neat. However, the growing popularity of higher grade feni has meant that *cazulo* is rarely produced apart from seasons when the cashew crop may have been affected by poor weather. The third grade feni has an ABV of between

40–50 per cent but is, consequently, much more expensive to buy. Some brands of feni contain additional flavouring such as cumin or cinnamon to add a spicier undertone.

Coconut feni is produced by much the same outdoor home distilling method but with sugar added to the coconut sap prior to distillation. One reason for the relative decline in coconut feni is that bleeding the bark of coconut trees sterilises the tree's fruit-producing potential and growers have found that the market for coconut feni is too small to afford such a sacrifice.

One of the main obstacles in cashew feni being granted Geographical Indicator (GI) status has been that there is little, if any, quality control or product regulation covering Goa's 4,000 or so mini-distilleries. As a result the market is flooded with cheap femi of poor (and in some cases dangerous) quality. Cashyo and Big Boss are good quality triple-distilled feni produced by reputable companies. There have been several reported cases in recent years of Western tourists being fatally poisoned by drinking cheap imitations that have been mixed with battery acid and other chemicals to strengthen their alcohol content.

TASTING NOTES: One distinctive feature of cashew feni is the pungent odour that accompanies the drink when a fresh bottle is opened and poured into a glass. The smell (bouquet would be stretching things a little) is vaguely reminiscent of iodine and this has put off the Western tourists who flock to Goa. Other than the overpowering odour, cashew feni is slightly sour tasting with a faint nuttiness and is best drunk either as a shot or with simple mixers (*see* cocktails below).

GOOD FOR: Disabusing would-be travellers of the notion that there is a mystical experience awaiting on the beaches of Goa and it is time to up sticks and go and join the hippy trail. All that awaits them is a filthy hangover.

TRIVIA: The smell of feni is said to be so difficult to wash from a glass that in most bars in Goa the drink is served in special feni glasses set aside for solely that purpose. Travel blogs also attest that getting drunk on feni is not to be encouraged as the next morning's hangover is accompanied by the same pungent odour as the alcohol is sweated out through the pores.

As part of the push to widen the appeal of the drink and garner GI status, the Goan authorities invited several prominent European liqueur connoisseurs to develop a method whereby the smell could be smothered or extracted during the distillation process. This caused some controversy in the regional press in Goa, with many locals incensed by what they felt to be an attempt at westernisation of their traditional drink. The contingent of European experts however, finally came to the conclusion that the smell was an inimitable aspect of the drink and that to eliminate it would destroy feni's uniqueness in the spirits world. It is entirely possible that this was just a smokescreen to cover the fact that nobody could work out how to get rid of the stench.

Indian Summer

2.5cl feni
2.5cl Cointreau
2.5cl lemon juice
orange juice
ice cubes

Stir feni, Cointreau and lemon juice over ice cubes in a highball glass and top up with orange juice.

Kissy Kissy

2.5cl Feni
2.5cl Chambord
1.5cl Cointreau
ice cubes
twist of lime juice

Pour Feni, Chambord and Cointreau into a cocktail shaker with ice, shake and strain into a cocktail glass, add a twist of lime.

ISRAEL

Sabra

DESCRIPTION: Chocolate and orange-flavoured liqueur with an alarming colour.

BACKGROUND: Sabra, the bestselling liqueur in Israel, was developed by the Bronfman family in 1963 and distributed through their multi-national distillery and drinks business Seagram. Sabra was developed very much on a whim by Samuel Bronfman and its origins are entwined with Bronfman family mythology.

Samuel Bronfman and his two brothers Harry and Abe were first generation Russian/Jewish immigrants whose father, Yechiel, had been a successful tobacco farmer in Moldova. The Bronfman family fled Imperial Russia in 1889 to escape the anti-Semitic Tsarist regime of Alexander III and settled in Canada. After an initial period of hardship working on the construction of the Northern Canadian Railway,

Yechiel started a number of small businesses, including a firewood delivery firm and a horse trading network. In 1903 the Bronfman family borrowed money to buy the Anglo American Hotel in Emerton, Manitoba. Over the next decade the Bronfmans' business grew to the extent that they bought up and developed several hotels in Manitoba and spread their business interests to other Canadian states such as Ontario and Saskatchewan.

Although often dogged by anti-Semitic suspicion from local authorities and rumours that, despite their outwardly respectable appearances, their hotels were little more than fronts for illegal gambling and prostitution dens, Samuel Bronfman and his two brothers continued to prosper. In 1916 the temperance movement that had been spreading across Canada reached Manitoba and Ontario, spelling disaster for the Bronfmans' business interests. Samuel Bronfman, realising that the sale of alcohol was by far the most lucrative aspect of the business, started producing and distributing cheap whisky. Although the sale of hard liquor was prohibited in Manitoba and Ontario, it was not illegal to 'import' liquor from state to state. The Bronfmans skilfully took advantage of this legal loophole by setting up mail order companies in different states and literally buying and selling their own products to themselves for sale in their various establishments and to 'private' customers.

By 1918 most Canadian provinces had adopted prohibition laws and begun to tighten regulation of the movement of alcohol from state to state. Despite new laws causing the closure of the Bronfmans' mail order scams, Harry discovered that the sale of alcohol was still permitted in the state of Saskatchewan for medicinal purposes. This proved a watershed moment in the brothers' career as they promptly filed for and received a licence to create a wholesale drug company which they named the Canada Pure Drug Corporation (CPDC). Although the CPDC provided small quantities of medicinal alcohol to pharmacies and hospitals, its main activities were confined to importing vast quantities of contraband whisky which were re-bottled and sold on the black market.

By the time prohibition started in the US in 1920, the Bronfman brothers had stockpiled huge warehouses full of illegal liquor along the border between Saskatchewan and North Dakota, which provided perfect access to the American market. Not content with the huge turnover from their import and export business, the brothers' next move was to start their own distillery business to produce and bottle their own stock.

Not surprisingly, the Bronfmans' position at the forefront of the underground liquor business began to attract the unwanted attentions both of federal enforcement agencies in Canada and organised crime organisations in the US. Indeed, 1922 proved to be something of an *annus horribilis* for the Bronfmans as they were indicted for non-payment of income tax by the Department of National Revenue after it discovered that it hadn't received a tax return from the family for over five years. Then, at the height of a crime wave surrounding bootlegging and rum running, Paul Mattoff, a family member, was murdered outside one of the Bronfmans' warehouses close to the US border. Matoff's killers were never found and various theories exist as to the circumstances behind the crime, from bungled robbery to gangland hit. The ensuing public outcry that the case provoked was enough for the local authorities to effectively ban the brothers from continuing with their export activities.

Samuel Bronfman moved to Montreal and set up a new distillery business. Quebec was one of the few Canadian provinces to have resisted prohibition laws (state prohibition lasted less than a year before being repealed due to intense public pressure) and provided the ideal environment in which to try and legitimise the family business. After a couple of years' consolidation, Samuel Bronfman purchased what would become the famous Joseph E. Seagram Distillery in Waterloo, Ontario, and began to plan carefully for the end of prohibition in the US.

When the end finally came, however, the Bronfmans again found themselves under investigation for various federal offences relating to tax evasion, company fraud and false accounting. After a protracted and complicated legal battle the brothers were acquitted, but were hit with a $3 million bill from the US Treasury Department for unpaid customs and excise tariffs.

As the Seagram brands began to corner a significant slice of the US liquor market the Bronfmans embarked on an assiduous public relations drive to obscure their prohibition era misdemeanours. Samuel Bronfman began setting up various charitable foundations and became a major figure in the Canadian Jewish Congress which provided considerable support for Jewish refugees and Holocaust survivors after the Second World War. In this context, the creation of Sabra, a kosher liqueur created to be drunk on traditional Jewish holidays, can be seen as part of the Bronfman family's concerted attempts to reconnect with their roots whilst disguising some of the far less palatable aspects of their history. 'Sabra' is a word with close Zionist associations and is often used to describe Jewish people born in the State of Israel.

In 1967, Samuel Bronfman was made a Companion of the Order of Canada, the highest rank in the Canadian Honours system awarded to individuals for their humanity, philanthropy and services to the nation. By his death in 1971, the mythology of the powerful but benign immigrant family made good was well established. It is only fitting then that the Bronfmans' spectacular rise in the first half of the twentieth century should be mirrored by a sudden and ignominious decline at its close.

Seagram continued to prosper throughout the 1970s and 80s, at one point owning over 250 brands. Under the chairmanship of Edgar Bronfman, the company started an aggressive expansion programme into areas other than liquor production and distribution. This, in hindsight, proved to be the start of the downfall of the Bronfman dynasty. After becoming involved in a protracted bidding war for the oil company Conoco, Seagram became saddled with considerable debts. Edgar Bronfman took over as chief executive and began to indulge his passion for the entertainment business by buying up controlling interests in Universal Studios and music companies MCA and Polygram in 1995. These investments proved to be disastrous for Seagram and within five years the entertainment operations were acquired by French media conglomerate Vivendi and the once-famous drinks company was auctioned off to various bidders such as Coca-Cola and Pernod Ricard. In 2003, the Bronfmans' 'home-made' Jewish liqueur Sabra was sold to the Carmel Winery Corporation in Israel where it is currently produced. After making their fortune with shrewd manipulation of market forces, it is ironic that the Bronfman empire should disintegrate when those same forces turned against it.

TASTING NOTES: Sabra is very much a drink for chocolate lovers, or more specifically lovers of orange flavoured chocolate. It is thick and gloopy with the orange notes more prominent on the nose than on the palette. Serving Sabra at room temperature brings out more of a citrus tinge.

GOOD FOR: Sabra makes excellent boozy chocolate truffles. Add a couple of splashes into a simple mix of melted chocolate, butter and whipped cream and then leave to chill for several hours until set.

TRIVIA: Seagram sponsored The Grand National between 1984 and 1991. In the last year of their sponsorship the race was won by a horse named Seagram, owned by property tycoon

Sir Eric Parker. Sir Eric bought the horse on the advice of an associate at the Racehorse Owners Association, Steven Smith. Smith was also a non-executive vice-chairman of Seagram. Strange coincidence?

One lasting legacy of the Bronfman empire can be found in the form of architect Ludwig Mies van der Rohe's modernist skyscraper on Park Avenue, New York. The Seagram Building was commissioned by the Bronfmans in 1954 to act as the company's US headquarters and is a protected New York landmark. The Seagram Building was sold off with the rest of the Seagram assets in 2003 and is currently owned by property tycoon Aby Rosen.

Wonka Bar

2.5cl Sabra
2.5cl vodka
1cl Chambord

Shake ingredients in ice and strain into a cocktail glass, garnish with chocolate shavings and float a fresh raspberry on top.

Jewish White Russian

3cl vodka
2.5cl Sabra
3cl fresh milk
ice cubes

Pour vodka and Sabra over ice, add fresh milk and stir.

ITALY

Dumante

DESCRIPTION: Pistachio-flavoured liqueur, produced in Italy primarily for the American market and soon to be available in Europe.

BACKGROUND: Dumante (or Dumante Verdenoce to give it its full title) is the brainchild of two Louisville lawyers Howard Sturm and Paul Paletti. Sturm is an amateur wine buff and connoisseur whose passion was for seeking out unusual and hard-to-find drinks on field trips to Europe. On one such trip to southern Italy, Sturm was searching for a walnut-flavoured liqueur when he came up with the idea of producing a pistachio-infused liqueur. To Sturm's astonishment, there were no pistachio liqueurs on the market and, after enlisting the help of business partner and fellow drinks enthusiast Paletti, the two men set about creating a world first.

Sturm made several trips back to Italy to research and develop his product, eventually joining forces with a small drinks distillery in Sicily, the centre for pistachio-farming in Italy where the fertile, mineral-rich soil of the slopes of Mount Etna provide the perfect environment for cultivating the pistachio crop.

Sturm and Paletti spent four years developing their product and refining the recipe, trying some two hundred different variations of the drink before finally settling on a combination they were happy with. Dumante combines high grade, locally distilled molasses liqueur with a pistachio infusion and natural vanilla essence. The liqueur is hand-made in small batches and aged in traditional oak barrels to provide a rich, golden natural colouring. Sturm and Paletti aimed their drink at the high end luxury spirits market and designed a unique, flat, five-sided glass decanter in which to package their product.

Clever marketing strategies such as setting up Dumante MySpace and Facebook pages, sponsoring culinary and arts events and promoting music concerts, mean the brand has grown steadily over the three years since its launch. Although still only available in selected parts of the US, Dumante won the gold medal at 2010 San Francisco World Spirits Competition and plans are in the pipeline for a European launch during the next two years.

TASTING NOTES: Dumante has a fantastic nose to it, with hints of almond and marzipan which bring to mind Battenberg cake. The pistachio flavour is nicely balanced with the vanilla essence and, although sweet, the use of molasses liqueur in place of vodka or cognac as the base alcohol has greatly reduced the sugar content.

GOOD FOR: Fine dining. The Dumante website contains some fantastic, delicious sounding recipes incorporating their liqueur, including Dumante glazed scallops and candied pistachios with foie gras, fried figs and Dumante sauce.

Lounge Lizard

2.5cl Dumante Verdenoce
2.5cl rum
cola
ice cubes

Pour the shot of Dumante over ice followed by shot of rum and top up the glass with cola.

Italian Royale

2.5cl Dumante Verdenoce
2.5cl Chambord
champagne or cava

Blend Dumante and Chambord in a champagne flute and stir, add sparkling wine of your choice to top up. Garnish with a fresh raspberry.

Limoncello

DESCRIPTION: Southern Italian speciality made from locally grown lemons around the Gulf of Naples.

BACKGROUND: There are various conflicting histories of limoncello, among them the claims by the company Limoncello de Capri to have been the originators. Late in the ninteenth century, an innkeeper named Vincenza Canale is said to have developed a lemon infused drink as a digestive aid to give to the patrons who dined in her restaurant. It proved so popular that Señora Canale soon began commercial production of the drink that she named limoncello. Canale is also credited with instilling the practice of giving dinners a shot of Limoncello *gratis* at the end of their meal, a tradition that survives in most restaurants in the area today.

There are hundreds of small producers of limoncello dotted around the Amalfi coastline and the Sorrento peninsula, all with their own tales of ancestral recipes. In all likelihood however, the drink developed along similar lines to Maraschino in that it was initially produced by nuns creating medicinal fruit based drinks known as '*rosoli*'. Whereas Dominican monks in Dalmatia used locally grown wild cherries, the nuns of the Bay of Naples chose the plentiful fruits of the local lemon groves.

There have been frequent claims by the locals on the island of Capri that the only true limoncello derives from them. Subtle variations in the flavour of the drink depend on the type of lemon used in production, or more specifically the area where the lemons are grown. Sorrento lemons are plump and bright in colour and are much sweeter than ordinary lemons, so much so that local children pluck them from the trees in the groves and eat slices of them as if they were oranges, as they lack the usual acid sourness. A few miles away in Amalfi, the lemons have a much stronger scent which aids the infusion of the alcohol and contain hardly any pips.

Recent European Union regulations have decreed that in order for a product to call itself limoncello it must be produced from Sorrento lemons. Any similar product using lemons grown elsewhere should be labelled 'limoncino'. The limoncello producers of southern Italy, stretching from Amalfi to Sicily, have steadfastly refused to pay any attention to this nonsense, especially as limoncello has become very popular in southern California where there are several companies currently producing it for the domestic US market.

TASTING NOTES: The strange thing about limoncello is that it tastes almost entirely different in situ from how it does anywhere else other than in mixed drinks. Sitting outside on the terrace of a small, family run restaurant in Sorrento marvelling at the view across the Bay of Naples, having just consumed a delicious plate of clam linguine, it tastes divine. Served ice cold in chilled, quaintly decorated, tiny porcelain cups, the lemon zing is sweet but not overpoweringly so and if made well, the grain alcohol provides just the right amount of warming afterglow.

However, in almost any other situation it tastes like watery lemon curd that somebody has splashed a bit of vodka into. It is possible, that the limoncello that is sold to tourists is not the same as the limoncello they serve in Sorrento restaurants, although that doesn't account for why they give the good stuff away free. Unless it is all part of a sly confidence trick.

GOOD FOR: Impressing dinner party guests with your own home-made traditional Italian style *digestivo*. Limoncello, after a few trial runs, is extremely easy to make. There is a near foolproof recipe included in the appendix.

TRIVIA: Pop singer Avril Lavigne claims to have written her song 'I Can Do Better' whilst drunk on limoncello, going as far to then try and recreate the 'creative moment' by getting drunk on the drink again when she came to record it for her third album, 'The Best Damn Thing'. The song contains the following heart-felt vow in the second verse: 'I will drink as much limoncello as I can, and I'll do it again and again.'

Posh Lemonade

4cl limoncello
1cl lime juice
6cl champagne

Gently blend the lime juice into the limoncello by stirring and then top up glass with champagne.

Blueberry Puppy Dogs

10cl limoncello
2cl lemon juice
2cl simple syrup (sugar and water mix)
1 cup of blueberries
10cl carbonated water

A delightful frozen cocktail for hot summer afternoons. In a blender or with a hand blender mix the blueberries with lemon juice, simple syrup and limoncello until they form a rough slush. Add the carbonated water and freeze for two hours. When ready to serve thaw for twenty minutes and spoon the icy slushy mixture into tall glass. Drink with a straw and maybe garnish with a sprinkle of chopped blueberries.

Maraschino

DESCRIPTION: Clear cherry liqueur sold in traditional straw covered bottles.

BACKGROUND: The original recipe for maraschino dates back to the early sixteenth century where it is believed to have been developed by the apothecaries of the Dominican monastery in the city of Zara in modern Croatia (known today as Zadar). By the eighteenth century several distilleries had sprung up around Zara to produce the liqueur, which was highly prized by the royal courts across Europe. Napoleon Bonaparte is known to have been an ardent admirer of maraschino which he drank as a *digestif* at state banquets.

The most famous brand started life in Zara in 1821 when a consul to the king of Sardinia, Girolamo Luxardo, opened a distillery in the city. Luxardo's maraschino, perhaps on account of his considerable diplomatic connections, soon established itself as the premier brand at the European courts. Francis I of Austria bestowed 'royal privilege' upon the drink with other monarchs soon jumping on the bandwagon. George IV sent the Royal Navy to Zara to collect a huge consignment of maraschino, partly to stock the royal cellars and also to be delivered as gifts to the governors of the British islands of Malta and Corfu. Popularity of maraschino continued throughout the ninteenth century amongst aristocrats and royalty with successive British monarchs such as Queen Victoria and George V numbered amongst its admirers.

With demand for their product far outstripping supply, Girolamo Luxardo's grandson Michelangelo built a huge modern factory near to the port in Zara in 1913. At the end of the First World War, the kingdom of Dalmatia was divided up with Zara absorbed into the Italian state. The Luxardo

Company continued to flourish up until the Second World War when blanket bombing by the Anglo-American alliance literally raised Zara to the ground. The port was particularly badly hit with the Luxardo factory completely destroyed. Following the end of German occupation, Dalmatia was overrun by Communist partisans from neighbouring Yugoslavia under the command of General Tito. Tito's troops ransacked what little was left of Zara and systematically murdered any remaining Italian citizens who hadn't fled into exile. Among those were killed were several members of the Luxardo family including the company head Nicolò Luxardo and his wife Bianca who were brutally tortured before being forcibly drowned in the harbour.

The one surviving member of the family, Giogio Luxardo, escaped to northern Italy where he eventually rebuilt the family distillery near Padova in 1947. The Luxardo brand remains a family run business and has branched out into other liqueurs such as Sambuca and limonchello.

TASTING NOTES: Maraschino, not surprisingly, has a strong aroma of cherries and this gives the anticipation of the drink itself being cloyingly sweet. Although, there is a sugary, syrupy quality to maraschino, some brands, Luxardo amongst them, use crushed cherry pips during the maceration and distillation processes and this adds a pleasant almond-like finish.

GOOD FOR: The Hemingway Daiquiri, a cocktail classic that the writer modified to his tastes whilst living in Cuba in the 1930s (*see* recipe below). Hemingway once said that if he was going out drinking in Havana he'd drink six of these of an evening but if he went out to get drunk he'd drink twelve.

Hemingway Daiquiri

4cl white rum
2.5cl lime juice
2.5cl maraschino
2.5cl sugar syrup
lime zest

Mix in a cocktail shaker with ice, strain into a cocktail glass and garnish with shavings of lime zest.

Saratoga Handicap

5cl cognac
2.5cl maraschino
2.5cl pineapple juice
2.5cl lemon juice
splash of angostura bitters

Combine the ingredients in a cocktail shaker with ice, strain and pour into a cocktail glass.

Tuaca

DESCRIPTION: Super sweet brandy-based liqueur infused with vanilla essence, lemon and orange.

BACKGROUND: Legend (or Tuaca's marketing department at least) holds that Tuaca was originally created in tribute to Lorenzo de' Medici, the de facto ruler of the republic of Florence during the latter part of the fifteenth century. Lorenzo the Magnificent, as he is known, was something of a polymath: an accomplished poet and artist; a fervent supporter and patron of Italian Renaissance painters such as Michelangelo and Botticelli; a skilled hunter, horseman and horse breeder who competed in Siena's infamous Palio horse race and, most significantly of all, a brilliant diplomat and politician. Although there is little, if any, historical evidence to back up Tuaca's claim, there isn't anything to refute it either and it is more than likely, given Renaissance developments in the sciences, that the Medici court would have employed apothecaries and alchemists to produce elixirs.

The real story of the Tuaca brand begins 450 years later with Florentine businessman Alfred Neri's purchase of a run-down distillery in the Renaissance port city of Livorno, some forty miles from Florence. Neri bought the distillery chiefly as a tax write-off and to provide work for his two workshy sons-in-law, Gaetano Tuoni and Giorgio Canepa. Initially the Tuoni e Canepa Company, as it was named, produced cheap imitations of other Italian liqueurs and spirits such as sambuca and ponce. Unbeknownst to Senore Neri, his two sons-in-law had more ambition than he had hitherto given them credit for and began experimenting with new products. Their early attempts at innovation were not very successful, particularly a mix of Tuscan brandy, vanilla, orange and fresh milk which they sold under the name 'Milk Brandy'. Undeterred, Tuoni e Canepa removed the milk, refined the blend of ingredients and released a rich, sweet liqueur which they named 'Touca' by combining the first syllables of their surnames.

The drink developed a cult following among American servicemen stationed in Italy after the Second World War and led to the company developing a lucrative export business with the US from the late 1950s onwards. By the 1960s, the name of the brand had evolved into Tuaca on the grounds that the largest importer in the US kept writing the name of their product down incorrectly on the shipping invoices.

In 2004, Tuoni e Canepa was taken over by American drinks giant Brown-Forman, producers of Jack Daniels and Southern Comfort. Initially Brown-Forman continued production at the factory in Livorno but in 2010 the Livorno plant closed, with manufacturing of Tuaca switching to Brown-Forman's home in Tennessee.

TASTING NOTES: Tuaca is best served chilled in single shot glasses. Syrupy, sweet and sticky, vanilla is the principal flavour with hints of orange and a chocolate finish.

GOOD FOR: Tuaca is excellent when added to traditional Italian desserts such as Zabaglione with stewed pears.

Tuaca Crumble

5cl Tuaca
10cl apple juice
juice of half a lemon
ground cinnamon
slices of apple
ice cubes

Shake Tuaca and apple and lemon juice in a cocktail shaker and strain into a tall glass over ice, dust with ground cinnamon and garnish with apples slices.

Italian Job

Created by writer and drinks guru Simon Difford in honour of the cult film.

2.5cl Tuaca
2.5cl amaretto liqueur
2.5cl cranberry juice
italian red wine
crushed ice

Shake Tuaca, amaretto and cranberry juice, pour over crushed ice in a tall glass and fill to the top with red wine.

JAPAN

DESCRIPTION: Home-brewed rice wine that is technically illegal in Japan.

BACKGROUND: Doburuku is the name given to home-brewed rice wine. In English, rice wine is often referred to as *'sake'* whereas in Japanese the word *sake* is a generic term for any alcoholic drink. Doburuku is a specific form of rice wine that is brewed according to a simple, centuries-old technique.

The origins of doburuku are unclear. Classical Japanese texts such as the *Kojiki* ('The Record of Ancient Matters') make reference to early brewing techniques such as *kuchikami no sake*, a method similar to that deployed by South American tribes where nuts and grains were chewed in the mouth to react with saliva enzymes and then spat into a pot and left to ferment (*see* **Chicha**). During the Asuka period (between the sixth and eighth centuries) the brewing of rice wine had evolved into more or less the form in which it exists today: the fermentation of rice grains in water with kōji fungus. At this time the production of rice wine was primarily for use in spiritual and religious ceremonies and was not widely consumed by the general population.

For the next 500 years only abbots in the temples and ancient shrines were permitted to brew rice wine and hence its consumption was severely restricted. By the age of the Daimyos (feudal warlords) in the sixteenth century, new techniques and technologies imported from other parts of Asia and from Europe had led to developments in fermentation and distillation. However, despite these developments, the production of rice wine and other forms of alcohol was still very much in the hands of religious and spiritual leaders.

It was not until the Meiji Revolution restored imperial rule to Japan in 1867 and dismantled the centuries-old feudal system that the restrictions on brewing were relaxed. A new law was created that enabled anyone to set up their own brewery and an estimated 30,000 *sake* houses sprung up in Japan within two years of Emperor Meiji's ascent to the throne. It could be argued that this explosion of *sake* mania was indicative of the huge shifts occurring in Japanese society at the time as the country developed rapidly into a highly industrialised, capitalist culture. The Japanese authorities soon realised the revenue potential of the *sake* industry and started to impose heavy taxation on the producers. Inevitably the sheer volume of producers could not be sustained by the market and gradually the number of industrial *sake* houses decreased to around 8,000 by the end of the nineteenth century. The majority of the most successful breweries were set up by landowners who grew rice crops. The production of rice wine was a very profitable source of alternative revenue, especially during years of over-abundance. It was common practice for housholds to brew their own doburuku at this time, a fact that irked the Japanese authorities as they had no effective way of taxing home-brewed rice wine.

The advent of the war with Russia between 1904 and 1905 provided the perfect opportunity for the Japanese government to outlaw the home brewing of doburuku. The supposed reason behind the ban was to discourage alcoholism during a time of national crisis but this was merely a smokescreen to raise more revenue for the war effort through increased taxation. At the time of the war, over 30 per cent of Japan's annual taxation was supplied by the *sake* industry and the rationale was that by banning home brewing, more tax could be collected through greater sales of industrially-produced *sake*. The ban has never been repealed in Japan although it is, to a large extent, unenforceable, and the authorities generally turn a blind eye to small family or farm-based producers.

During the Second World War severe rice shortages forced the Japanese authorities to restrict the brewing of rice wine. In order to keep their industry alive the producers began to add a grain-based alcohol to the rice mash during fermentation and diluted the wine before bottling. This practice continued after the war and now 75 per cent of all *sake* produced in Japan contains additional alcohol.

The rice harvest occurs in September and October and according to a tradition thousands of years old, none of the rice is to be eaten until an elaborate harvest festival has taken place to give thanks for the year's crop. These events are known as doburuku festivals and usually consist of colourful processions to a nearby temple or shrine where cups of locally-made doburuku are offered to the gods and passed round and drunk in abundance. Although, as already stated, the brewing of doburuku is outlawed, each of the rice growing regions is given special dispensation to brew and consume rice wine specifically for the harvest rituals. These harvest festivals are often riotous affairs with 'binge' doburuku drinking going on for several days and nights.

TASTING NOTES: The quality of doburuku varies greatly. As with home-brewed wine or beer in Europe, no two batches are ever exactly the same if made in the traditional artisanal manner. Where doburuku varies from industrially-produced *sake* is that it usually has an opaque off-white colour and due to no alcohol being added during fermentation, a smoother milky finish. A recipe for making doburuku is included in the appendix.

GOOD FOR: Eastern mystical religious ceremonies; goes well with raw fish cakes.

TRIVIA: Doburuku was brewed on Japanese airbases during the Second World War. Pilots earmarked for kamikaze missions were given several bowls of their squadron's homebrew to drink prior to boarding their planes.

COCKTAIL RECIPES

The following recipes require premium *sake* but homemade doburuku could be substituted if it has been carefully filtered to make it as clear as possible.

Fuji Sunset

5cl rice wine
2.5cl maraschino
2.5cl orange juice
2.5cl lemon juice

Pour ingredients into a cocktail shaker with ice, gently shake and strain into a cocktail glass.

Divine Wind

'Divine wind' is the literal English translation of the word '*kamikaze*'.

5cl rice wine
2.5cl limoncello
2.5cl vodka
2.5cl lemon juice
slice of fresh lemon

Pour vodka, limoncello and lemon juice over ice, stir and top up with rice wine, garnish with a slice of lemon.

Midori

DESCRIPTION: Bright luminous green melon-flavoured liqueur used in many modern cocktails.

BACKGROUND: Midori is a relatively new drink, first launched onto the market in a blaze of publicity in 1978. It is produced by the Japanese drinks manufacturer Suntory who are one of the oldest producers and distributors of alcoholic spirits in Japan. Suntory originally specialised in producing various imitations of Western spirits, particularly malt whiskies.

The company had humble beginnings when in 1899 a young entrepreneur named Torii Shoten opened a small wine store in Osaka. Shoten originally intended to sell only imported wines but his interest turned to producing his own with the launch in 1907 of Akadama Port Wine.

Shoten's wine experiments and store became a success, and in 1924 he founded the Yamazaki Distillery, a factory dedicated to producing Japan's first Scottish-style whisky. Shoten chose as the site for his factory an area of Kyoto that was famous for the quality of its water (sixteenth-century philosopher and tea master Sen no Rikyū had built his famous tea rooms close to the site) and enlisted the help of Masataka Taketsuru. Taketsuru had studied organic chemistry at the University of Glasgow and worked in several Scottish distilleries; he was well versed in production and maturation techniques. Taketsuru's influence played a key part in the company's development and in particular the launch of their flagship brand Suntory Sirofada Whisky, a single malt derived from Scottish models.

Taketsuru left the company in 1934 to set up his own distillery which would later develop into the Japanese drinks brand Nikka (now owned by the Ashali beer corporation). Shoten continued to develop his passion and brought several different whisky varieties onto the market before production ceased during the Second World War. After the war, Suntory Sirofada was re-launched with the famous advertising tag line 'Drink Tory's [whisky] and Go to Hawaii'. The idea of travel abroad in the post-war period of austerity was merely a pipe dream for most Japanese and the company cleverly exploited this by suggesting that Suntory had a happy-go-lucky sophistication just beyond their reach. Quite why drinking an imitation Scottish whisky made in Japan should evoke the carefree lifestyle of Hawaii is a mystery, but the campaign worked and resulted in a sharp rise in sales.

By the early 1970s Suntory was keen to exploit the growing popularity of cocktails and started product development on a sweet fruit liqueur. After seven years of trials the company finally settled on a honeydew melon liqueur named Midori which was first launched in the US in 1978.

TASTING NOTES: The first thing to note about Midori is the extraordinary colour; it really does look alarmingly like Fairy Liquid with a not dissimilar consistency to boot ('*midori*' is the Japanese word for 'green'). Drunk neat it is overly sweet and sugary with hints of melon and a faint tang of ginger. The problem is that melon-flavoured products, even organic, naturally infused ones, always taste slightly artificial. Where Midori is most effective is in a huge range of modern cocktails.

GOOD FOR: Hands that do dishes…

TRIVIA: Suntory held their 1978 launch party in New York at the Studio 54 nightclub right at the height of the disco craze. This strategy of positioning Midori as the drink of choice for clubland's beautiful elite was further enhanced by product placement in the film *Saturday Night Fever*, most notably when the camera settles on a huge advertising billboard for the drink in Times Square during the closing credits.

The Universe

Created for the launch party at Studio 54 to highlight Midori's versatility in mixed drinks, The Universe won the prestigious US Bartenders' Guild Award in 1978.

1.5cl vodka
1.5cl Midori
1.5cl Dumante
1.5cl lime juice
5cl pineapple juice
crushed pistachio nuts

Pour ingredients into cocktail shaker with ice, shake for thirty seconds, strain into a cocktail glass and garnish with a sprinkle of crushed pistachios. The prolonged shaking allows the pineaple juice to froth a little and gives the drink a pleasant creamy head.

Japanese Slipper

5cl tequila
2.5cl Midori
2.5cl fresh lime juice

Pour ingredients into a cocktail shaker with ice, strain into a cocktail glass with a salted rim.

LITHUANIA

Krupnik

DESCRIPTION: Clover honey and herb liqueur made since the sixteenth century and popular with the aristocracy.

BACKGROUND: Krupnik, or krupnikas as it is known in Lithuania, is a blend of grain alcohol, herbs and clover honey. The drink is believed to have been developed in the sixteenth century by Benedictine monks at the Niaśviž monastery. The medieval city of Niaśviž is in modern-day Belarus, but in the sixteenth century it was part of the the Grand Duchy of Lithuania. The monastery was constructed on the orders of the city's ruler, Mikołaj Krzysztof Radziwiłł, a prince of the Holy Roman Empire. Krzysztof Radziwiłł was a statesman, scholar and patron of the arts and sciences. In 1582, he undertook an extensive pilgrimage to the Holy Land which he recorded in a diary that was published in 1601. Amongst the many cultural and civilising developments that Krzysztof Radziwiłł gleaned from his travels was an understanding of alchemy which he passed on to the monks to aid the creation of their 'elixirs'.

Various versions of krupnik exist in Lithuania and Poland. Poland's iconic Baczewski Distillery of Lwów (*see* **Altvater**) produced a very popular version of the drink in the ninteenth century. A high-quality version of krupnik is produced today by the Sobieski distillery in Gdańsk.

In Poland it is traditional to drink krupnik on Christmas Eve. The drink is served warm, having been gently heated in a pan with added cloves and cinnamon in a tradition similar to mulled wine. A recipe for creating your own krupnik can be found in the appendix.

TASTING NOTES: Served chilled, krupnik is basically a sweet flavoured vodka with a pleasant spicy kick to it. When served warmed; the blend of honey, cinnamon and nutmeg come to the fore and the aromas released by heating are more fragrant and enticing.

GOOD FOR: Banishing the winter blues by warming up a cupful as a delicious nightcap.

TRIVIA: Polish soldiers were given krupnik as part of their rations during the Second World War. They were advised not to drink it, but to use it as an emergency antiseptic dressing for flesh wounds.

Polka Dot

2.5cl krupnik
2.5cl Bison Grass Vodka
2.5cl lemon juice
5cl fresh cream
a few dashes of Blue Curaçao
ice cubes

Mix the krupnik, vodka and lemon juice in a cocktail shaker with some ice, slowly pour in the cream and shake. Strain into a tall glass with ice and gently drop in some spots of Blue Curaçao.

Belarusian Revolution

4cl krupnik
2.5cl Kahlua
cola
ice cubes

Pour Krupnik and Kahlua over ice cubes and top up with cola.

MONGOLIA

Kumis

DESCRIPTION: Ancient drink made from fermented horses' milk.

BACKGROUND: Kumis has been produced by the people of the Central Asian Steppes (a vast region ranging from the Caspian Sea into central China) since the fifth century BC. The practice of fermenting mare's milk originated amongst the various nomadic tribes of the area. Ancient Greek historian Herodotus (c. 484–425 BC) describes the fermenting of mare's milk by a tribe of Scythians (Persian nomads) in his classical text *Histories*. The Scythians are observed painstakingly milking their horses and pouring the collected liquid into vast wooden vats that are then stirred by blind slaves and left in the sun to ferment; finally, the top is skimmed off and drunk.

Mare's milk is a rare commodity, partly due to the difficulties in obtaining raw unpasteurised milk from a lactating horse.

Industrial production of kumis often substitutes cows' or yaks' milk which is more plentiful and then adds sucrose or whey to fortify the milk to approximate the consistency of mares' milk.

The process of producing kumis occurs entirely naturally. Mares' milk contains roughly 40 per cent more lactose than cows' milk prior to fermentation. By agitating the milk and heating it gently (to about 80 degrees centigrade) a natural bacteria (lactobacilli) is released converting the lactose into lactic acid which react with the yeasts and sugars to produce a mildly alcoholic, carbonated drink.

The original method for producing kumis involved putting the mares' milk into a horse hide container called a '*saba*' and either dangling it above the doorway of a '*yurt*' (a felt, tent-like structure common to Central Asian nomadic peoples) or strapping it to a saddle on a horse. Tradition holds that if neighbours or passers-by saw a '*saba*' dangling outside a yurt, etiquette required them to punch it a couple of times to agitate the contents. The saddle method provided agitation through the exertions of a hard days riding and hunting on the plains and rewarded the hunter with a fresh, relaxing drink of kumis on his return to camp.

One explanation for the development of kumis in Mongolia is that over 85 per cent of the population suffer from lactose intolerance. The high lactose composition of mares' milk renders it virtually undrinkable but this can be circumvented by fermenting the lactose into acids whilst retaining the high protein values. In the late ninteenth and early twentieth centuries, kumis developed a doubtful reputation as a miracle cure for a variety of ailments such as anaemia, bronchitis and tuberculosis. This led to the creation of 'Kumis Cure' resorts in southern Russia where the terminally ill could check in for rest and relaxation and were prescribed regular quantities of kumis.

The prominent American physician William Gillman Thompson discusses kumis resorts in his book *Practical Diatetics* (1905) but suggests any favourable results occurring in patients staying at these resorts was as much to do with the weather as being administered kumis. Anton Chekhov checked into one such resort in August 1901 seeking relief from chronic tuberculosis. Chekhov found little relief from the four bottles of kumis a day he was prescribed to drink but duly noted that his weight had gone up twelve pounds during a two-week stay.

Kumis is usually served as a welcome drink to visitors and poured from the bottle into small ceramic bowls called *piyalas*. It is customary also to strain the sludgy dregs that collect at the bottom of the *piyala* back into the bottle.

TASTING NOTES: Kumis is very low in alcohol content, typically no more than 2.5 per cent ABV (although stronger, distilled kumis is produced in some countries). The sensation of drinking kumis is not as unpleasant as it may sound from the description of the drink above. It is a little like drinking slightly fizzy, watery sour cream which has a faint metallic after tang. No doubt stronger varieties have a stronger aftertaste and this is probably not altogether a good thing.

GOOD FOR: Mares' milk is an absolutely world class laxative so a glass of kumis, regardless of other claims to its health benefits, should at least provide relief from constipation.

TRIVIA: 'A Confession' (1884), Leo Tolstoy's autobiographical essay on religion and the meaning of life, describes the following remedy for artistic burnout: 'I fell ill, mentally rather than physically, threw up everything, and went away to the Bashkirs in the steppes, to breathe fresh air, drink kumys, and live a merely animal life.'

President George W. Bush became the first U.S President to visit Mongolia in 2005. Bush's hosts treated him to the traditional Mongol welcome by inviting him into a yurt and offering him a glass of kumis. As Bush was supposed to be a recovering alcoholic and therefore teetotal it is unclear if he accepted the drink.

White Mongol

4cl vodka
10cl kumis
ice cubes

Variation of the White Russian but using kumis instead of ordinary milk. Simply pour over ice cubes and stir.

The Golden Horde

4cl light rum
10cl kumis
ice cubes

Similar to the White Mongol except the substitution of light rum adds a yellowish effervescence and a nice caramel-like sweetness.

THE NETHERLANDS

DESCRIPTION: Premium grain-based spirit flavoured with juniper oils and considered to be the original precursor to gin.

BACKGROUND: Genever (also spelt jenever) is a traditional alcoholic spirit that is native to the Low Countries and areas of Northern France. A form of genever is thought to have first appeared in Holland towards the end of the sixteenth century but was used purely for medicinal purposes. The Dutch physician and scientist Franciscus Sylvius is often credited with creating genever around the 1650s. Dr Sylvius was experimenting with treatments for kidney disorders and developed a diuretic treatment using grain alcohol flavoured with juniper oils. Prior to Sylvius' developments most grain alcohol was aged as the rawness of grain distillate was considered too harsh for general consumption. The addition of juniper oils, though, produced a strong tasting aromatic spirit which was considerably cheaper to produce and required little aging.

The commercial production of genever began to take off in 1664 when the Bols family distillery released its first genever on to the market. The Bols family had set up what is now considered by many to be the oldest distillery in the world in Amsterdam. The distillery *'het Lootsje'* or 'The Little Shed', as it was known, was originally situated outside the city walls but such was the expansion of Amsterdam as a key trading port that by 1612 the city had swallowed it up. Lucas Bols (born 1652) took over the running of the company at the age of twelve and was largely responsible for developing it into the renowned trademark that it is today.

A large part of Lucas Bols' success was founded on the back of the Dutch East India Company, of which he was a major shareholder. The Dutch East India Company, or VOC, was set up by a cartel of powerful traders in 1602 and was given extraordinary powers by the States-General of the Netherlands (Dutch parliament). In addition to establishing and securing valuable trade routes to Asia and Africa, the VOC had the right to negotiate treaties with foreign powers, create colonial outposts and even wage war if it didn't get its own way (which it usually did). By the mid-seventeenth century the VOC had wrestled control of the lucrative spice trade from the Spanish and Portuguese and was less of a company and more of a huge floating colonial power in its own right. In addition to a fleet of over 150 merchant ships, the VOC also owned a flotilla of 40 warships and could call upon a private army of 10,000 soldiers.

The VOC was the first company to issue shares in the capital stock of their business interests and it was through purchasing this stock that Lucas Bols was able to gain a valuable foothold in the VOC's activities. Of particular advantage to Bols was the cheap and easy access to exotic herbs, fruits and spices which the company used in flavouring their genevers as well as in the production of imported recipes from the New World (*see* **Blue Curaçao**).

The company continued to expand throughout the eighteenth century but the Bols family dynasty came to an end with the death of Herman Bols in 1813. The Bols distilleries were sold on the condition that the name be maintained. Over the next 200 years the company changed ownership several times, acquiring and merging with various other drinks manufacturers. In 2000, French distillery giant Remy Cointreau bought Bols in a €510 million deal which helped to revive the company's flagging fortunes. The merger eventually led to a management buy-out in 2007 and the establishment of a new company under the traditional name of Lucas Bols B.V. In addition to their trademark genevers, Bols also produces a range of over thirty specialist liqueurs.

Genevers can traditionally be divided into two distinct forms of '*oude*' and '*jonge*' (literally 'old' and 'young') which relate to methods of production more than any sustained aging process. *Oude* is comprised of a blend of distilled malt wine infused with juniper oils and other herbs. Some brands of *oude* are aged in oak barrels for up to a year to give the spirit a yellow golden colour. *Jonge* is not aged at all and is double- or triple-distilled from refined grains to produce the malt wine base and then often blended with neutral spirit alcohol and less juniper oil to produce a lighter clear spirit. There are other 'fruit genevers' produced by some companies, with blackberry and elderberry being the most common flavourings but they are not, strictly speaking, genevers unless they contain a juniper infusion.

TASTING NOTES: *Jonge* genever, being multiple-distilled from refined grain mash (often a mix of grains such as barley and corn) bears more than a passing resemblance to a slightly juniper-flavoured form of high-grade vodka with tones of aniseed. By contrast, *oude* genevers, particularly those that have been aged in oak barrels (Bols Corenwyn is actually aged in used American bourbon barrels) has more malty tones similar to whisky and has a higher sugar content added during processing which makes it noticeably sweeter. It would be churlish to assume that genever has an identity crisis however. There are hundreds of small genever producers spread across the Netherlands and Belgium with many variations on the oude/jonge axis.

GOOD FOR: The *oude* and Corenwyn varieties of genever are traditionally bottled in beautiful handmade stone jugs and clay bottles which are highly collectable, look great in the drinks cabinet and could be reused for bottling homemade doburuku.

TRIVIA: The expression 'Dutch courage' relates specifically to genever and was coined by English soldiers and sailors in the eighteenth century. The popularity of 'Dutch Gin' led to the development of English Dry Gin as British distilleries attempted to replicate the flavours of genever.

Orange Collins

7.5cl oude genever
1.5cl Cointreau
3cl fresh lemon juice
2cl sugar syrup
Angustora Bitters
soda water
slice of fresh orange

Stir genever, sugar syrup, cointreau, lemon juice and a couple of splashes of bitters in a cocktail shaker with ice. Shake gently and strain into tall a chilled glass over ice, top up with soda water. Garnish with the slice of orange.

Holland House

A cocktail classic attributed to Harry Craddock, who worked at the Holland House in New York in pre-Savoy Hotel days.

6cl oude genever
2.5cl dry vermouth
2.5cl maraschino
twist of lemon juice

Shake with ice in a cocktail shaker and strain into a cocktail glass with a twist of lemon.

NORWAY

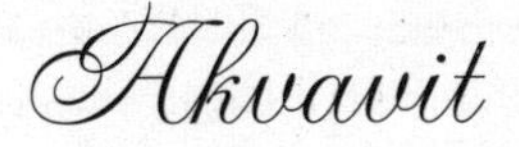

DESCRIPTION: Carroway and herb-flavoured *digestif*. This 'water of life' is often drunk with accompanying songs praising its virtues.

BACKGROUND: The name aquavit or akvavit derives from the Latin aqua vītae, meaning water of life, and is known to have existed in various parts of Scandanavia since the sixteenth century. A letter from Eske Bille, a Norwegian nobleman to Olav Engelbrektsson, the archbishop of Norway expounds the medicinal virtues of a local elixir produced by one of his apothecaries: 'Dear lord, will your grace know that I send your grace some water with Jon Teiste which is called Aqua vite and the same water helps for all his illness that a man can have internally.'

Akvavit is made in a similar way to vodka by producing a fermenting mash of grains and/or potato peelings, fermenting it with yeasts and then triple distilling to produce a neutral base alcohol. This base is then infused with a variety of different herbs and spices, the most prominent being caraway seeds and dill.

The rivalry between Scandinavian nations concerning their different styles and varieties of akvavit is intense. Swedish and Danish akvavits tend to be milder in flavour and lighter in colour, and some have caramel added as a sweetener. Norwegian akvavit is produced from a mash of potato peelings and aged in oak casks to provide a dark golden hue and increase strength.

One of the principle Norwegian brands is Linie Aquavit, which is aged through the novel expedient of transporting the barrels on long shipping journeys. This practice dates back to the blockade of Danish and Norwegian ports by the British during the Peninsular War. In 1805, a Norwegian merchant ship the *Throndhiems Prøve* set sail from Trondheim bound for Batavia, the capital of Dutch Indonesia. The journey was extremely perilous as the Royal Navy under the command of Admiral Lord Nelson was routinely attacking or capturing merchant ships in breach of the blockade. The *Throndhiems Prøve* was carrying a cargo of traditional Norwegian products such as salt cod, dried herring and barrels of akvavit. The ship arrived at Batavia on 21 December 1805, just in time for Christmas (the traditional time for akvavit to be consumed) but although the merchants had no problem offloading their fish products the Dutch colonialists were less enamoured with the akvavit as they had their own stock piles of Dutch genever. Consequently, several barrels were left unsold to be transported back on the long return journey to Trondheim.

When the ship arrived back in Norway on 11 August 1807 the crew made a remarkable discovery: the quality and taste of the akvavit had improved remarkably for its arduous travels. This gave rise to the theory that the rolling motion of the sea and the radical changes in temperatures had helped to meld the flavours and release otherwise hidden infusions. Thus, Linie Aquavit was born with a unique selling point: each oak barrel must be transported across the equator and back before bottling to ensure its quality remains constant. This practice continues to this day with Linie transported to Australia and back on large container ships. On the reverse of each bottle label is a stamp giving the name of the ship and the dates and times of its voyage.

Linie Aquavit has the classification of 'Noble Brandy' on account of aging in oak casks. The standard akvavit is aged for around sixteen months with special reserve varieties taking anything up to three or four years. Linie use a particular type of oak barrel which is imported from southern Spain and has typically been used for storing sherry. These Spanish barrels are believed to impart wine-like aromas and the rich dark colourings.

As stated above, akvavit is traditionally drunk at Christmas in Scandinavia and every year since 1988 Linie have produced a special yuletide akvavit with a unique recipe that changes year by year.

TASTING NOTES: There is a marked difference between various brands and styles of akvavit with the use of carroway seeds the defining ingredient. Classic Linie Akvavit has a rich colouring and alongside the keynotes of dill, carroway and coriander is a tender aniseed finish. Sweedish akvavit tends to be lighter with warming, almost chocolate-like tones on account of the caramel sweetener.

GOOD FOR: Swedish crayfish parties. It is a tradition in late summer for families living on or near the coast to celebrate the crayfish harvest by holding gatherings where fresh crayfish and cheeses are feasted upon and large quantities of akvavit are drunk. Ettiquette dictates that the host sits at the head of the table and determines when his or her guests can drink by proposing a toast; this involves raising his or her glass and shouting the word '*ska*!' The guests are then permitted to take a drink but cannot drink again until the host has given the signal. In between toasts traditional *snapsvisors* are sung, short whimsical drinking songs extolling the virtue of 'the water of life'.

Danish Mary

2.5cl akvavit
10cl tomato juice
2.5cl lemon juice
Worcestershire sauce
celery salt
Tabasco (optional)
ice cubes

Measure the ingredients into a high ball glass with ice and stir, sprinkle on a little celery salt and add some dashes of Tabasco if heat is desired. Do not shake in a cocktail shaker and strain as this tends to make the tomato juice foamy.

Girl Friday

Created by Hollywood actress Rosalind Russell and named after her most famous role as Hildy Johnson, the quick-witted newspaper reporter in the Howard Hawks film *His Girl Friday* (1940).

5cl akvavit
2.5cl dry vermouth
2.5cl lemon juice
ice cubes
slice of lemon

Blend the ingredients in a cocktail shaker with ice and strain into a cocktail glass. Garnish with the lemon slice.

Karsk

DESCRIPTION: Dangerously strong Norwegian grain-based alcohol that is drunk with lukewarm coffee.

BACKGROUND: Karsk is a legendary form of moonshine that is traditionally drunk with 'weapons-grade' strength coffee. The origins of karsk are fairly murky to say the least; Norse legends tell of Ragnarök, the epic battle of the gods in which the world will ultimately be submerged, only to rise anew and a perfect creed be born by two 'chosen ones'. The classic medieval text of Norse mythology, *Poetic Edda,* tells of a form of 'liquid fire' which proved to be 'the ruin of the gods' causing their fracas and eventual downfall. Although not cited specifically in *Poetic Edda*, karsk is often referred to euphemistically as 'The Ruin of The Gods' in Norway.

Karsk is moonshine in the strictest sense. It is traditionally made by fermenting potato peelings and grains with yeast in a mash and then distilling to produce high grade ethanol. This home-made, ostensibly illegal moonshine is always drunk with coffee. At Norwegian rock festivals it is common practice for strong coffee to be sold in half-cup measures with the expectation that the recipient will fill up his or her cup with whatever karsk they have managed to procure beforehand.

The ritual of drinking karsk is as follows: take a porcelain mug and half fill it with very strong filter coffee. Then drop a small coin into the coffee and ensure that you cannot see the coin in the bottom of the receptacle (if you can then the coffee isn't of the required strength). Once the coin is no longer visible to the naked eye, fill up the rest of the mug with karsk and stir until the coin is visible again. Allegedly, your karsk with coffee is now of the required balance and consistency.

TASTING NOTES: Any actual proper, regimented attempt at providing an acurate taste test for karsk would be an extremely dangerous endeavor. The alcohol by volume ratio can vary from anything between 12 per cent, equivalent to a medium bodied red wine, to 85 per cent, which is not only undrinkable but also extremely dangerous. In general, karsk isn't a drink to be recommended or even tried, as it will be impossible to know by smelling neutral grain alcohol exactly what you are drinking.

GOOD FOR: Filling up the paraffin lamp or soaking the coals for the barbecue.

TRIVIA: Lemmy, the lead singer of heavy metal band Motörhead, attributes the distinctive warts on his chin to drinking Norwegian moonshine i.e. karsk, whilst on tour with his band in the 1970s. On a subsequent trip to Norway in 1989, Lemmy was questioned about his claims on Norwegian television. 'I don't want to talk about that stuff, its filth, not even the roadies will touch it anymore' was his unequivocal response.

Karsk/Norwegian Coffee

There is only one way to drink karsk and that is with strong coffee. The following recipe substitutes vodka for Karsk as a more palatable and easy alternative and won't make you go blind.

7cl strong, fresh filter coffee
14cl vodka
cinnamon stick

Brew the coffee and vodka and then transfer to a saucepan and heat gently over a low flame with a cinnamon stick until the alcohol starts to evaporate, allow to cool for a few minutes. Discarding the cinnamon, transfer to a large mug and add sugar or cream if desired.

SOUTH AFRICA

Amarula

DESCRIPTION: A rich, sweet, cream-based liqueur drunk in shots over ice as an accompaniment to after-dinner coffee or in a variety of cocktails.

BACKGROUND: The history of alcoholic drinks is littered with examples of concoctions created initially for medicinal purposes, until some bright spark discovers the often pleasing intoxicating effects of drinking just a little too much. Few drinks in the world can claim that their exhilarating properties were first discovered by the animal kingdom and that it took quite a while for the human race to catch on. This is, however, the case with Amarula cream.

Amarula is made from the macerated flesh of the fruits of the marula tree. The marula tree is indigenous to the sun-baked plains of South Africa and holds a quasi-mystical place in African folklore. The hare, a sly and merry prankster in

African folk tales, is said to have been kind to the elephant during a terrible drought. As a reward, the elephant gave the hare one of his tusks which the hare promptly buried in his garden. The marula tree grew at the spot where the tusk was buried bearing a magical fruit that could provide sustenance for the animals in times of famine. This tale was probably used to explain the ardent fondness elephants have for marula fruits which they consume in enormous quantities during the harvest season of late February and early March. However, zoologists studying the behaviour of plains animals have noted that the elephants tend to eat the fruit in large quantities when it is at its ripest, often leading to them becoming temporarily listless and noticeably unsteady on their feet – in short, drunk. The marula fruit is exceptionally rich in fructose (natural sugars) and a combination of this and the searing climate causes the juices of the over-ripened fruit to ferment into alcohol. As a drink this is just about as organic as one can get and it is odd that it wasn't until 1983 that the commercial possibilities of producing marula-based alcohol were first developed. The elephants, it seems, were well ahead of the game.

In 1983, Amarula was launched but didn't prove to be particularly successful, largely due to its rather harsh acidic tones. In 1989, noting the growing global cocktail culture and market, the Amarula brand re-launched as a cream liqueur. The brand has become phenomenally successful and is the second largest selling cream liqueur globally behind Baileys Irish Cream.

Amarula is unusual in that unlike traditional cream liqueurs it does not use whisky or brandy as its base but a variation of the original distilled Amarula spirit. The fruit is macerated into a pulp and then fermented using traditional wine-making practices. The wine is then distilled into the spirit and matured, brandy style, in oak casks for up to three years before blending with cream.

TASTING NOTES: An aroma that recalls creamy hard boiled sweets such as Werthers Originals, a throwback, no doubt, to gentler times. The initial taste is of butterscotch followed by some faintly fruity hints. It is extremely sweet and best used in cocktails.

GOOD FOR: The marula tree is also known as the 'Marriage Tree' and, according to local lore, has mystical and aphrodisiac properties when it comes to aspects of love. Keep a bottle around if dating and then, should your date pop in for a nightcap, you can impress them by reeling off all the ethical initiatives Amarula are involved with while you wait for 'The Spirit of Africa' to work its magic. Amarula is also very useful in cookery. The company website has a recipes section covering such delights as Amarula Caramel Cookies and Amarula Bread and Butter Pudding.

TRIVIA: As a global company, Amarula is refreshingly ethical. The marula fruit harvest is undertaken solely by local plains people and provides much-needed income to an impoverished and desolate area of South Africa. Amarula also fund education and development projects in the marula growing areas and are firmly committed to conservation and environmental initiatives. Touchingly, Amarula has ploughed over three million rand into an elephant conservation and research project at Natal University. A little thank you to the elephants for giving them the heads-up about the alcoholic potential of marula trees.

Rhino

2cl Kahlua
2cl Amarula
2cl Cointreau

Pour the shots in layers with the Cointreau resting on top and then set fire to it for no discernable reason. Extinguish and serve.

Sowetan Toilet

6cl banana liqueur
4cl Amarula
1.5cl cheap brandy
a dash of chocolate liqueur

Mix all the ingredients in a blender until smooth. The name is no doubt a reference to the fearsome colour of this cocktail.

SPAIN

Hierbas

DESCRIPTION: Golden-coloured herbal *digestif* popular on the Balearic Islands, particularly Ibiza.

BACKGROUND: The island of Ibiza, renowned as the party capital of the Mediterranean, where thousands of fun-seekers flock each year to spend long nights in the hip nightclubs and bars and long days recovering on the beaches, is the home of hierbas.

The origins of the drink are unknown. Early elixirs produced by apothecaries date back to a period when the island was an Imperial Roman outpost and these could then have been further enhanced by Islamic rule under the Moors in the eleventh century. The Moors introduced exotic spices to the island and it formed part of a link between North Africa and the Iberian Peninsula where the Moors had established a stronghold.

After a period of upheaval during the Crusades when the island was captured by just about anybody who happened to be passing on their way to the Holy Land, James I of Aragon conquered Ibiza in 1235 and the population reverted to Christianity. This led to a period of largely peaceful self-determination that lasted for almost 500 years, allowing the island to develop its distinctive and relaxed culture.

Hierbas in something akin to its current form is known to have been produced on the island for at least 200 years. The rural communities on the island were comprised of small autonomous *fincas* (farmsteads) and each of these took great pride in producing its own medicinal restoratives from whatever was at hand. This generally meant gathering wild roots, seeds, fruits, berries and herbs to macerate and infuse a blend of wine-based alcohol and molasses. This tradition of home-brewing on the island's *fincas* exists to this day, with many small producers operating as traditional cottage industries.

Towards the end of the ninteenth century, small companies began to spring up on the island to produce hierbas commercially. One of the oldest of these is the Mari Mayan family's business who set about refining and developing a rich herbal restorative that combined eighteen different ingredients. Local lore stands by the health benefits of hierbas and Mari Mayan is no exception with much of their publicity revolving around the use of rosemary essence to combat rheumatism and fresh thyme as a homeopathic remedy for chest infections. The brand Hierbas Ibcencas is ubiquitous on the island, stocked in virtually every bar and *bodega* (wine store) and emblazoned on giant billboards. The company also has an army of yellow vans that are more prevalent than taxis, scurrying from bar to bar and restaurant to restaurant replenishing supplies.

Mari Mayan Hierbas Ibcencas has recently been made available in the UK via a Leeds-based import franchise trading under the name 'Taste of Ibiza'. The product is now being marketed at the lucrative 18–25-year-old clubbing fraternity with a view to rivalling Jägermeister and other popular shooters.

TASTING NOTES: Mari Mayan Hierbas Ibcencas, although claiming to be carefully blended from eighteen ingredients is very heavy on the star anise with a faint juniper finish. The herbal notes are more prevalent in the nose with pungent hints of thyme in particular. Hierbas Ibcencas has an ABV of 26 per cent.

Other varieties of heirbas vary according to the ingredients used in the infusion; some are herbier, with mint used instead of anise. Many bars on the island stock 'straight off the farm' varieties that rest on the side of the bar in glass vats with a small copper tap attached. Herbs and spices can be seen floating inside. These traditional artisanal versions tend to be stronger and the quality and flavours can vary. Usually the barman will allow you to 'try before you buy' though and so fun can be had in comparing the different varieties and trying to ascertain the different infusions.

GOOD FOR: As an escape from the gurning club casualties crowding the beaches and the constant thumping dance music, some Ibiza tourist companies offer 'Make Your Own Hierbas' days out. These entail spending a day on a rural *finca* foraging for natural ingredients and then instruction on how to create different infusions and blends. A picnic or barbeque is usually thrown in and participants can bottle and personally label their own handmade hierbas to take away as a souvenir.

H Bomb

A rival to the club favourite Jägerbomb.

4cl hierbas
energy drink
ice

Fill a tall glass with a carbonated energy drink and ice and float hierbas on the top.

Spaced Out

4cl hierbas
2.5cl vodka
2.5cl Cointreau
lime juice
soda water
ice

Pour herbas, Cointreau and vodka into a cocktail with ice, shake for twenty seconds and strain into a tall glass over ice. Top up with soda and a twist of lime juice.

Patxaran

DESCRIPTION: Sloe-flavoured liqueur from the Basque Country of northern Spain.

BACKGROUND: Patxaran is a traditional artisanal liqueur that has been made in the Navarre region for centuries. It was originally developed for medicinal usage in the fifteenth century and rapidly spread around the Basque-speaking region of Spain with local farmers producing their own distinctive varieties. The first historical citation of patxaran states that it was served at a wedding banquet thrown in honour of the son of a Basque nobleman in 1418. The medical records of Monasterio de Santa María de Nieva in the Castilian city of Segovia cite the use of patxaran as an antacid and useful cure for digestive complaints which suggests that the usage of patxaran for medicinal purposes was not confined to the Basque region.

Patxaran's popularity as an after dinner *digestif* developed towards the end of the ninteenth century as producers first began to bottle and sell it. It was not until the 1950s that larger scale commercial production of the drink took off though, with the development of the Zoco brand, a company set up by the Velasco family who had a tradition of producing patxaran as a cottage industry dating back to the 1800s.

The essential ingredient in terms of flavouring is the sloe berry, which grows wild and plentifully in the region. Sloes are picked when semi-ripe as it is believed that these impart the best flavour and colouring. Mature or over-ripe berries lose their essential colouring agents during soaking and younger, under-ripe green sloes are considered too bitter to properly balance the flavour. Master producers subject wild sloes to a pinch test to determine their suitability. This entails squashing a sloe berry between thumb and forefinger and 'reading' the colour of the juice that squirts out. A ruddy, deep blood red is considered to be the ideal indicator of a particular blackthorn bush's suitability for harvest. The sloes are soaked in a wine-based alcohol that has been infused with anise for at least six months; some producers also add other flavourings such as coffee beans and vanilla pods or additional sugars to sweeten and round the bitterness of the sloes.

In 1987 patxaran production in the Navarre region was granted Denominacion de Origen by the EU and a regulatory body set up to administer quality control and strict guidelines in production techniques. Patxaran's popularity is gradually spreading beyond Spain, largely through increased tourism in the Basque region where Bilbao and San Sebastian have become popular destinations for travellers.

TASTING NOTES: Patxaran does not improve with age; in fact, quite the opposite is true, so a good patxaran should always be bottled in a dark green glass bottle as this helps to protect it from the light. Generally, most commercial patxaran have a sweet burst from vanilla, coffee or liquorice, with the sloes providing a more pungent bitter finish.

GOOD FOR: Basques believe that patxaran has anti-depressant qualities and taking a medicinal tot at morning and at night can reduce anxiety and stress and keep the inner demons at bay.

TRIVIA: The sudden burst in popularity of patxaran in Spain in the 1950s is believed to have been partially caused by Spanish soldiers on National Service under Franco being issued with bottles as part of their personal medical rations.

COCKTAIL RECIPES

Patxaran Republic

2.5cl patxaran
2.5cl crème de banana (Amarula Cream can be substituted)
2.5cl fresh lime juice
5cl pineapple juice

Blend all of the ingredients in a cocktail shaker with ice and strain into a cocktail glass.

Basque Coffee

2.5cl patxaran
25cl strong filter coffee
4cl fresh double cream

Pour the patxaran into a tall coffee glass, fill up with fresh coffee and stir, then float a layer of fresh cream on the top.

UNITED KINGDOM

Buckfast Tonic Wine

DESCRIPTION: Controversial fortified wine with high caffeine content that has a cult following in Scotland.

BACKGROUND: Buckfast Tonic Wine is produced by Benedictine monks at the Buckfast Abbey on the edge of Dartmoor National Park in Devon. The abbey itself is the only medieval abbey in the UK that has been restored to be used as a working monastery.

A monastery was first founded at Buckfast during the reign of Kind Cnut in the eleventh century. Positioned close to the bubbling waters of the River Dart, the site was chosen on account of its beauty and tranquillity as the perfect place to commune with God. Wild deer could often be seen drinking from the river and grazing in the leafy clearings; it is believed that the name Buckfast means 'deer safe' or deer sanctuary. This gentle, spiritual, pastoral idyll is as far removed as possible from the controversy that surrounds a drink that has become notorious in Scotland and synonymous with the phenomenon of anti-social behaviour.

The monastery itself underwent various changes during the Middle Ages. In 1147 the monks converted to the Cistercian order and the abbey was redesigned and rebuilt in stone. The Cistercian monks used areas of land around the abbey to rear sheep and set themselves up as wool producers and farmers. Up to the Black Death (1348–50) the abbey prospered but the advent of the plague caused the abbey to fall into disrepair and economic crisis.

In the fifteenth century the abbey was revived under the stewardship of William Slade who set about modernising it by setting up a school and maximising the abbey's commercial interests. By the sixteenth century the monasteries had become rich and powerful land owners and their influence upon their parishes, manors and communities was becoming a cause of some concern to the Crown. Between 1535 and 1539, King Henry VIII set about dissolving the monasteries and seizing their assets. The justification for issuing Deeds of Surrender was that the monasteries were riddled with corruption and had lost sight of their spiritual duties. In truth though, it was very much part of Henry's sustained battle with the Catholic Church and an estimated 1.5 tons of gold and silver plus numerous other treasures were seized along with huge areas of land.

Buckfast Abbey was dissolved on 25 February 1539 and over the next 200 years was left to fall into ruin. In 1800 a local landowner, Samuel Berry, bought the site and kept some of the original features but also removed large parts of the ruins to build a manor house on the site. By 1882 the site was owned by Dr James Gale who had the idea of returning the abbey to its original use. Dr Gale placed an advert in the Catholic newspaper *The Tablet* offering the site for sale or long-term lease. A group of exiled, homeless French Benedictines were sheltering in a temporary residence outside Dublin at the time and saw the advert. The monks sent a representative to meet with Dr Gale in Plymouth and on 25 October 1882 signed a lease. The first six monks soon arrived to start rebuilding the abbey to its former glory.

Once the monks had settled in their new home they began producing a medicinal tonic based on a recipe they brought with them from France. This involved importing Spanish mistellas wine as the base ingredient and fortifying it according to a secret process. For the next forty-five years the monks produced their tonic in relatively small quantities which they sold through the abbey shop and by mail order. The tonic wine was intended to be used as a medicinal restorative and the label contained the following instructions: 'Three small glasses a day, for good health and lively blood'. In 1927, James Chandler, a London wine merchant visiting the abbey had a chance conversation with the then abbot, Anscar Vonier. The abbey had recently had its licence to sell their tonic wine revoked and the J Chandler company offered to distribute their product for them. The monks modified their recipe to make the tonic more palatable by diluting the alcohol content and sweetening it. The result is more or less the Buckfast that is sold today (give or take the addition of additives and caffeine) although the claims to be a medicinal tonic no longer appear on the bottle label.

The reasons behind Buckfast's phenomenal cult following in Scotland and certain areas of Glasgow in particular are unclear, although it is likely to be largely the result of social and economic factors. The popularity of the drink is particularly prevalent in what has been unflatteringly referred to in the media as 'Ned Culture'. 'Ned' stands for 'non-educated delinquent' and relates to a sub-culture of white, mostly unemployed, urban working-class youths. 'Neds' are associated with the modern pantheon of anti-social behaviour including petty crime, drug abuse, football hooliganism, gang violence and, most pertinently, underage drinking. Buckfast became the drink of choice for the 'Ned' as its potent mix of high alcohol content and caffeine is considered to create a quick and easy 'high'. Buckfast is also relatively cheap in comparison with other forms of alcohol and a single bottle will suffice in getting even the most battle-hardened drinker tipsy.

With anti-social behaviour never far from the top of the political agenda, particularly in the tabloid press, it was inevitable that the Buckfast phenomenon would soon attract the attention of politicians. Firstly, Helen Liddell when Secretary of State for Scotland, publicly denounced Buckfast as a major cause of social deprivation in a speech in 2005. She was swiftly followed by the Scottish Justice Minister Cathy Jamieson, who put forward proposals for off-licences in her constituency to be barred from selling Buckfast. At this point Buckfast seemed to be on the receiving end of a witch-hunt with Scottish Health Minister Andy Kerr stating in a radio interview on 23 September 2006 that Buckfast was 'an irresponsible drink in its own right'.

Not surprisingly, Buckfast's distributors were livid at these attacks upon their product and the J Chandler Company issued a statement outlining possible legal action for what they considered to be clear 'defamation' and concerted efforts to undermine their rights protected under the free distribution of tradable goods legislation. One of Chandler's legal threats was to sue the Scottish executive for loss of earnings should the Buckfast ban be enforced, but in an ironic twist which can only have embarrassed the politicians further, sales of Buckfast actually increased markedly in Scotland during the 2005–6 controversy.

In January 2010 a BBC Scotland documentary, *The Buckfast Code*, explored the links between the drink and petty crime in Scotland. According to the BBC's research, between 2006 and 2009 over 5,000 crimes in the Strathclyde area had some link to the perpetrators consuming Buckfast and over 40 per cent of young offenders at the Polmont Institute were regular Buckfast drinkers and had been drinking before committing their respective offences. These research findings were strenuously denied by both the monks of the Buckfast Abbey, who had up to this point remained bemused by the fuss their tonic wine was causing, and again by J Chandler Company, who pointed out that severe social deprivation in the areas the studies were carried out had been common for generations.

TASTING NOTES: Buckfast has a slightly sherry-like, yellow/brown hue reminiscent of harsh expectorant. The main flavours on the nose are of hand rolling tobacco with a faint tinge of coffee. It tastes almost exactly like cheap, flat cola that someone has mixed with cooking sherry. The cola taste is accounted for by an extraordinarily high caffeine content of on average 280 milligrams per bottle, which roughly equates to the same as eight cans of Coca Cola.

GOOD FOR: Enriching the lexicon of modern idiom and slang. Few drinks have inspired as many humorous euphemisms and nicknames as Buckfast which is referred to in Scotland as, among other things: 'Commotion Lotion', 'Wreck Da Hoose Juice' and 'Bend-Yer-Dick Broth'.

TRIVIA: An episode of the comedy show *Rab C. Nesbitt* is devoted to Buckfast. In the episode, Glasgow's self-styled drinking philosopher embarks on a spiritual pilgrimage to the Buckfast Abbey in Devon.

The Buckshake

5cl Buckfast Tonic Wine
10cl milk
1 chopped banana

Blend milk, banana and Buckfast in a bowl with a hand blender and pour into a tall glass.

Wreck Da Hoose Punch

50cl strong white cider
25cl Buckfast Tonic Wine
10cl vodka
25cl blackcurrant juice
crushed ice
sliced apple and lemon

Mix all the ingredients in a punch bowl by stirring with a wooden spoon and add a bag of crushed ice. Leave to stand for fifteen minutes and ladle into glasses.

Drambuie

DESCRIPTION: Whisky-based spirit liqueur flavoured with honey and herbs.

BACKGROUND: The legend of Drambuie dates back to the Jacobite rebellion of 1745 and the flight of Charles Edward Stuart, aka Bonnie Prince Charlie. After the exile of James II to France in 1688 and the ascension to the throne of the protestant William of Orange, widespread discontent spread amongst the catholic clans of Scotland loyal to the Stuart dynasty.

The Jacobite uprisings began in earnest with the coronation of George I, which firmly cemented the House of Hanover's right of succession to the throne of Great Britian and Ireland. Charles Edward Stuart, the grandson of the deposed James II, was born in Rome in 1720 and was to become a figurehead for Jacobite attempts to wrestle back the throne. On 2 August 1745 the small frigate *le Du Teillay* landed on the island of Eriskay carrying Charles Edward Stuart and seven clansmen; their intention was to unite the Jacobite clans and march on England to claim the throne.

At first the 'Young Pretender' had some success in raising his army; crucially, he was able to call upon the allegiance of clan Chieftain Iain Dubh MacKinnon and several hundred of his warriors, plus an assortment of Irish and French sympathisers. The Jacobites moved south towards the border but stiff resistance from George I's forces under the command of the Duke of Cumberland and an absence of vital reinforcements forced them to retreat.

The final confrontation took place on Culloden Moor on 16 April 1746. Jacobite losses were considerable and the heart of their army was routed. A hefty reward was offered for the capture of Bonnie Prince Charlie and he was forced into hiding, protected only by a small band of loyal supporters. Chief amongst the prince's aides was Captain John MacKinnon who assisted him in a series of narrow escapes from the king's forces.

When finally the prince reached relative safety he is said to have rewarded John MacKinnon for his bravery by presenting him with a bottle and the recipe for his own personal '*eau de vie*' which he carried with him at all times. MacKinnon returned to his clan heartland on the Isle of Skye where he was eventually captured. He was taken to London and imprisoned only to be released two years later by royal pardon.

According to Skye folklore the drink that Bonnie Prince Charlie bequeathed to John MacKinnon became the basis for the development of Drambuie, which was further refined and developed by successive generations. Although on the face of it the story sounds like a convenient cultural and historical peg to hang Scotland's premier liqueur brand on, there is actually some historical evidence to back up the claims. The prince was brought up under the protection of the king of France, Louis XIV, and would have been more than acquainted with the fashion for after-dinner *digestifs* and herbal restoratives. Bonnie Prince Charlie is known to have carried with him on his travels a personal medicine cabinet that is preserved and on display at the Royal College of Physicians in Edinburgh. The cabinet contains a collection of bottles of plant essences and tinctures in addition to scales and measuring devices, all of which suggests an interest in creating medicinal elixirs. *The Lyon In Mourning*, a collection of letters and oral history relating to the life of Bonnie Prince Charlie, was published in the ninteenth century and contains John MacKinnon's personal account of his friendship with the Prince and their escapes from capture.

By the 1870s 'dram buidhe', or the yellow dram on account of the additional saffron and honey added to the whisky blend, was being sold in the Broadford Inn on the Isle of Skye and the landlord, John Ross, patented the name Drambuie. A relative of John MacKinnon, Malcolm MacKinnon, whilst working for a wine trader in Edinburgh, persuaded the widow of John Ross to sell him the patent and the first commercially-produced bottles of the liqueur were produced by W. MacBeth and Son Wine Company in 1909.

Due to the increase in excise tax on whisky and falling sales, the MacBeth Wine Company met with financial difficulties and in 1914 the MacKinnon family brought out the company and renamed it The Drambuie Liqueur Company.

Throughout the twentieth century the company continued to grow and prosper and is now an established global brand. Remarkably, the company has remained in private ownership with the 'secret' recipe of Bonnie Prince Charlie passed down through the matriarchal line of the MacKinnon family, a tradition started by Malcolm MacKinnon's wife Gina.

TASTING NOTES: Drambuie is much stronger than most liqueurs on account of its whisky base but deceptively so. The sweetness of the honey tones is well-balanced by the hints of saffron and other herbs and the whisky base is beautifully smooth. It is sometimes described as 'Men's Baileys' as it is best served neat in shots over ice.

GOOD FOR: A Highland coffee. A take on the classic Irish coffee but with a shot of Drambuie substituted at the base, blended with warm filter coffee and then a layer of double cream floated on top.

TRIVIA: Doctor Samuel Johnson and his biographer James Boswell stayed on Skye with a relative of Captain John MacKinnon during a tour of the Highlands in 1777. Boswell recorded in his diaries that he and Johnson were generously served with a local 'golden dram' that Johnson was much taken with and sat up drinking late into the night. It is likely that this 'dram' was an early version of the MacKinnon family recipe for Drambuie.

COCKTAIL RECIPES

Rusty Nail

2.5cl Drambuie
2.5cl single malt Scotch whisky
dash of lemon juice
slice of lemon

Pour Drambuie and Scotch over ice, add a couple of dashes of lemon juice and garnish with a slice.

La Dolce Vita

2.5cl Drambuie
7.5cl champagne or cava
grated nutmeg

Add Drambuie to a chilled champagne glass, top up with sparkling wine and grate a little nutmeg on the top as a garnish.

UNITED STATES

Hpnotiq

DESCRIPTION: Blend of vodka, cognac and tropical fruit juices. Bright sky blue colour gives appearance of containing no natural ingredients. A sensation on the New York club scene.

BACKGROUND: A friend of mine works as a development scientist for a multi-national manufacturer of slightly dubious sugary yogurt products. Some years ago he hit upon the idea of producing a blue drink, specifically a blue beer and was convinced that it would sell, primarily on the grounds of its colour. 'People love blue!' he would decree with a certitude bordering upon evangelical fervour. It became something of a long-standing joke – Phillipe, a lovable and gregarious Frenchman and his 'concept' of blue drinks. Phillipe's various prototypes for '*Les Bleu Biere*' were largely undrinkable and he eventually lost heart in the project and he went back to his day job of producing vitamin-enhanced dairy drinks of questionable nutritional value. However, history has proved Phillipe right through the phenomenal success of Hpnotiq. It seems people do, after all *love blue*.

In 2000, Raphael Yakoby, a Georgian-born émigré living in New York was walking through Bloomingdale's department store looking to buy some expensive designer fragrance for his wife's birthday. Dazzled by the array of brightly-coloured, translucent bottles of dizzying design, Yakoby, a self-employed wine importer and distributor, hit upon the idea of producing a designer drink packaged in an eye-catching bottle. Yakoby and his wife teamed up with Nick Storm, a former music industry publicist and promoter, and set about developing the product. After various attempts at blending different combinations themselves in the kitchen of the Yakobys' New York apartment, a wine industry acquaintance put them in touch with a small family distillery in France run by Gilles Merlet, a producer of high grade cognac. The resultant blend of triple-distilled vodka, cognac and fruit juice concentrate was then infused with food colouring to give it its distinctive clear blue appearance.

Delighted with Merlet's creation, Storm and the Yakoby's set about aggressively launching the drink to the trendsetters in New York. Having failed to sell the concept to major drinks manufacturers and running out of money, Yakoby and his wife sold their apartment to fund their decision to go it alone. Storm and Yakoby, quite literally, took the drink to the streets by pestering the city's clubs and bars to sell it through a series of promotional events and parties which utilised Storm's music industry contacts. The big break came when hip hop impresario P Diddy agreed to sell the drink in his restaurant chain Justin's. Suddenly the bright blue liqueur in a bottle that would look more comfortable on a bathroom shelf than a bar optic was 'the drink' to be seen supping in all the hot places.

Such was the success of Hpnotiq that Storm and Yakoby soon found themselves in demand from style magazines and media companies eager to sell the story behind the drinks success. Yakoby's subsequent claims that the drink is based on a family recipe passed down from his Georgian ancestors initially threatened to derail the Hpnotiq express. Gilles Merlet, understandably irritated by the lack of recognition he had received for his part in the drinks creation, started legal proceedings against Yakoby and Storm. Meanwhile Yakoby, a keen amateur poker player, sold the franchise to American distillery giant Heaven Hill. As the saying goes, 'you've got to know when to hold them, and know when to fold them'.

TASTING NOTES: Fruit-based, blended liqueurs tend to be favoured by the sweet-toothed drinker. Likewise any drink coloured as alarmingly as Hpnotiq usually betrays a syrupy quality that offends the more discerning palate. Hpnotiq is a surprise then in that it isn't actually as sickly tasting as it looks. Aromas of pineapple and mango betray a false impression and the fruit juices (Yakoby has always refused to reveal exactly what fruits are used) offer a tartness that goes well with the vodka base and the subtle hints of sweet cognac.

GOOD FOR: Impressing middle-class white suburbanites who claim to 'know their hip hop'. Also very useful for producing flashy cocktails with semi-pyrotechnic effects.

TRIVIA: At the height of its hipness celebrities were falling over each other in a rush to be seen with a bottle of 'blue juice' in their hands. George Clooney was an early advocate and R Kelly opened his stint at the BET music awards with the words 'First, we're going to pop open the bottle of Hip-Hop-not-tick.' Name-checked by various recording artists including Lil Kim and Fabolous, the former won the race to be the first to come up with her own familiar catch phrase: 'Let's get hypnotised!' a reference to her penchant for drinking Hpnotiq mixed with vintage Moet and Chandon champagne.

Hpnotiq Hulk

50ml Hpnotiq
50ml cognac

Layer over ice in a rocks glass and let the drinker stir it up to watch the transformation as the drink changes colour.

Blue Devil

40ml Hpnotiq
20ml dry vermouth
10ml malt whisky

Combine Hpnotiq and vermouth over ice in a rocks glass; drizzle the whisky over the top.

APPENDIX: RECIPES

These recipes are relatively simple and fun to make but it is worth considering that every care should be taken to sterilise equipment properly when undertaking the fermentation process. If something looks or smells strange, don't give it a try to see what happens, chuck it down the sink and cut your losses.

Doburoku

The following recipe is designed for the doburoku beginner and as such has been simplified as far as possible. Once the basics have been mastered further experimentation can take place using different types of yeast and refining the Moto (starter culture). There is a wealth of bulletin boards and websites devoted to the joys of *sake* brewing, each offering handy tips and different methods to try out and explore.

The tricky part to begin with is acquiring the magic ingredient of rice wine making, namely koji-kin spores. Koji-kin is the bacterium that grows on rice which produces the enzymes to turn starches into sugars that can react with the yeasts to produce alcohol. The resulting malt-rice is called kome-koji. Some specialist Asian markets sell the spores dehydrated in small 10 or 20 gram packets or it can be purchased via mail order on the internet (occasionally supplies turn up on eBay). It is also possible to find ready-made i.e. pre-inoculated tubs of kome-koji in the fridges of specialist Asian shops and supermarkets but this is very rare in the UK

The following recipe should produce about three litres of doburoku at approximately 18–20 per cent ABV.

PART ONE: CREATING KOME-KOJI

Ingredients

400g short grain rice
1tsp koji-kin dried spores

Equipment

bamboo steamer
large saucepan
sieve
large stainless steel container
cotton cloths
10l metal or ceramic brewing bucket with lid (plastic ones can be used but need to be carefully sterilised)
filtering equipment

Instructions

Wash the rice thoroughly for several minutes under running water and leave to drain for thirty minutes. Cook the rice carefully in a bamboo steamer. It is advisable to place a piece of thin cotton fabric in the base of the part of the steamer containing the rice to ensure that there is no contact between the rice and the boiling water. Once cooked, allow the rice to cool to room temperature and put into a stainless steel container. Sprinkle on a level teaspoon of Koji-kin spores, gently stir through the rice, cover with damp cotton and leave in a warm place for about two days. During this period, agitate the rice by gently stirring at spaced intervals four or five times (approximately every ten hours). About halfway through creating this basic Moto you will notice a pungent smell of sweaty socks emanating from the mixture. Do not be alarmed: this is a good sign. After two days the rice should be covered in fine, white, wispy fibres. It is essential to use your kome-koji as soon as possible before it starts developing all sorts of other bacterias. The Kome-koji is quite volatile and it is important to check that the cheesy sock smell has not turned to a mouldy, musky smell as this may suggest the presence of other, possibly unhealthy bacteria.

PART TWO: SAKE A-GO-GO!

Ingredients

1.5kg short grain rice
4l cold, dechlorinated and filtered water
5g brewing yeast (champagne yeast from a homebrew shop is recommended but beer yeast will work)
1tbsp lemon juice

Instructions

Armed with your magic kome-koji it is time to get down to business. Wash the rice thoroughly for several minutes and leave to soak in cold water for at least two hours. Drain thoroughly with a sieve. Steam the rice as above; this may well have to be done in batches and leave to cool to room temperature. Sterilise the brewing bucket with boiling water. Dissolve the lemon juice into the water (the water can be prepared in advance by using a water filter and then leaving the water to stand for twenty four hours for the chlorine to evaporate). Add the kome-koji to the brewing bucket and stir thoroughly and then add the cooled steamed rice and stir again. Sprinkle in the yeast, stir thoroughly and cover with the lid. Store at room temperature away from direct sunlight.

Initially the rice will absorb all of the water but within forty-eight hours will start to break down into a white slushy mixture. Pay your doburuku mash a visit at least once a day and give it a thorough agitation by stirring. Within two to three weeks the first fermentation cycle will have finished and the mash is ready to be filtered. Filtering can be quite a time consuming business. Old filter coffee makers are useful; sterilise the basket first with boiling water and then spoon the mash a little at a time into filter paper and wait for the clear liquid to dribble through. If you are making a sizeable batch of doburuku this can take some time. Another method is to place the mash in nylon straining bags or cheesecloth and suspend it above a container such as a large brewing bucket. Once the filtering has been done the doburuku can be bottled and drunk almost immediately as it is sweeter when at its freshest; however, if stored in a refrigerator, it will improve for settling for a couple of weeks and become drier in flavour.

Additional Considerations

To increase the strength of your doburuku a second fermentation period can be added after the first by adding additional steamed rice and sugar to the mash and leaving to ferment for a further two weeks; this will also make the drink considerably sweeter when finally filtered. One aspect to be wary of is the possibility that there may still be yeast elements fermenting after bottling. As an additional precaution it is possible to semi-pasteurise doburuku by heating in a saucepan to roughly 145° centigrade for a few minutes (be careful not to overheat as this will impair the flavour). In addition to experimenting with the use of different types of yeast it is also possible to make a dry version of doburuku by using a higher quantity of citric acid. Citric acid powder can be easily obtained from chemists and should be added either to the original mash in place of lemon juice or at the start of the second fermentation period if brewing stronger doburuku.

Krupnik

This traditional Polish/Lithuanian liqueur makes a good winter alternative to mulled wine, although care should be taken when heating it over a gas burner.

The krupnik improves considerably the longer it is left for the sediment to settle before the final filtering stage so it is advisable to plan a few weeks in advance if considering making some for Christmas.

Ingredients

1 small cup (approx 20cl) of pure, organic clover honey
25cl filtered dechlorinated water
4 cinnamon sticks
6 cloves
zest of one blood orange (pesticide free)
2 split vanilla beans
50cl vodka (Polish vodka would add a touch of authenticity)
nutmeg

Equipment

large saucepan
glass demijohn with stopper
zester
fine grater
filtering equipment
storage bottles
siphoning tubes

Instructions

Gently bring the dechlorinated water and honey to the boil in a large saucepan, carefully stirring with a wooden spoon to dissolve the honey. Some froth may form on the top as it bubbles and this needs to be skimmed off. Once the honey has blended with the water add the cinnamon sticks, split vanilla beans and fine grate some nutmeg and the orange zest. When zesting the orange it is recommended that a hand zester is used and be careful not to include any of the white pith.

Cover the saucepan and simmer on a low heat for twenty minutes and then leave to cool and stand for one hour. Put the saucepan back on a low heat and gradually add the vodka a little at a time, stirring gently. Once the mixture starts to boil and all the vodka has been stirred in, remove from the heat and leave to cool. Filter the mixture a little at a time through filter paper. As suggested in the doburuku recipe, coffee filters are useful for this but it could be done straight into the demijohn with a funnel and filters available in homebrew and wine making stores. Place an airtight stopper in the demijohn and store in a cool place away from sunlight or heat for two to three weeks. Once the remaining sediment has settled, siphon off into an appropriate storage bottle.

Fragolo Strawberry Liqueur

This recipe is for an Italian-style Fragolo but can be adapted to use with other fruits and berries. Raspberries and blackberries work well or a mixture of different fruits. For a sharper, fruitier flavour experiment try using different ratios of fruit and sugar. This recipe takes very little actual preparation and quite a lot of waiting around for the liqueur to set but is well worth the wait.

Ingredients

350g large wild/organic strawberries
2 split vanilla beans
350g granulated sugar
350ml vodka
10cl dechlorinated filtered water

Equipment

glass demijohn with stopper
filtering equipment
sieve
large ceramic or stainless steel bowl

Instructions

Carefully wash and pat dry the strawberries, removing the stems. Slice the strawberries into quarters and put them into the demijohn with the sugar water and split vanilla beans. Pour in the vodka and seal the container with an airtight stopper. Give the demijohn a good shake and store in a cool dry place away from sunlight. Leave the strawberries to steep in the mixture for at least one month, agitating the demijohn daily with a gentle shake and swirl. After the steeping period, sieve the mixture through a wire mesh into a large bowl and pass the resulting liquid through filter paper. Bottle the filtered liqueur and put somewhere to set down for at least six months.

Limoncello

This recipe is very simple and produces impressive effects. The lovely lemon hue of this drink can't fail to impress guests and makes a lovely refreshing long drink if mixed with soda or tonic. For a slightly sharper tang try adding the zest of a couple of limes to the lemons. The choice of lemons is important. If possible source large Italian lemons for authenticity but any large lemon will do as long as it is unwaxed and preferably organic.

Ingredients

10 large organic unwaxed lemons (2 unwaxed limes optional)
75cl vodka
50cl filtered dechlorinated water
250g granulated sugar
lemon oil
thumb sized piece of peeled fresh ginger root

Equipment

demijohn with airtight stopper
storage bottles
zester
large ceramic or stainless steel bowl
sieve

Wash the lemons thoroughly and gently scrub them with an abrasive brush or scourers. Use a zester to zest the lemons; this should be done as carefully as possible to ensure that none of the white pith just below the skin gets into the zest as this will affect the flavour. Put the zest into a large bowl and pour on the vodka, stir, cover and put in a warm place for twenty-four hours. Stir the mixture and pour into a demijohn with a funnel, making sure to spoon in any zest left in the bowl, add the root ginger, seal with an airtight stopper and give the demijohn a shake and a swirl. Store the demijohn in a cool, dry place away from sunlight for four to five weeks. Agitate the mixture every day by giving it a gentle shake. After a month or so the vodka will have turned bright yellow and the zest will be pale and translucent; the limoncello is now properly infused. Filter the liquid through a sieve into a large bowl to remove the zest but keep the zest to one side discarding the ginger root.

Make up some simple syrup by heating the water and sugar in a saucepan and stirring constantly until all the sugar is dissolved. Pour the syrup through the sieve containing the zest and collect in a bowl and leave to cool. Once the syrup has cooled, stir it through the lemon-infused vodka and pour into storage bottles. Leave the limoncello to set in a dry place for a further two to three weeks and then transfer to a freezer. Limoncello is best served ice cold as a shot, combined in cocktails or used in cooking.

Pimms

The quintessential English summer drink, the Pimms Fruit Cup (or No1 Cup) actually started life as a stalwart accompaniment to shellfish in a nineteenth-century London oyster bar run by James Pimms. Pimms developed the drink as a digestion aid by blending a gin base with herbs, spices and quinine and garnishing with fresh fruit. The drink was served in a small tanker, known as a Number One Cup. The classic Pimms recipe as it is drunk at various events on the 'summer' circuit (Wimbledon, Henley Regatta, Glyndebourne etc) mixes

Pimms with mint leaves, English-style fresh still lemonade (not the grimly sweet bottled variety) and various sliced summer fruits. The alcohol content of Pimms has been reduced over the last twenty years and the recipe and taste of the drink moderated as a result. It is however possible to blend your own version of the Pimms gin base which has a stronger kick and is closer in authenticity to James Pimms original 'gin sling'.

Mix the following ingredients in a large jug
2 parts gin (Plymouth or Hendrick's is recommended)
2 parts red vermouth (or Dubonet)
1 part orange liqueur
1 part sweet port
healthy splash of Angostura bitters

add crushed ice, torn mint leaves and slices of strawberry and lemon and top up with fresh, chilled, still lemonade.

Chicha de Jora

Chicha de Jora is a traditional alcoholic beverage of the Andean region of South America. Traditionally it is made by fermenting *jora*, sun-dried Peruvian corn. Understandably, *jora* is quite tricky to get hold of in the UK, although packets of sun-dried corn can be found in specialist food shops. It is however possible to make a version of Chicha de Jora by cultivating sprouting sweetcorn and mixing with pearl barley. There are no hard or fast rules to producing *jora*, it is one of the world's great artisanal homemade drinks and experimenting with different spices and flavourings is part of the fun. Firstly though, in the absence of any dried *jora* the following process for sweetcorn acts as a worthy substitute.

Brewing Jora

In order to make 8 litres of chicha you will need approximately 500g of sprouting *jora*. Depending on the size of the corn cobs this will probably equate to at least a dozen cobs. The cobs need to be hung in a warm dry place (an airing cupboard would be good for this) for about two weeks until the kernels have dried and started to shrivel. Extract the kernels from the cobs and soak in cold water for forty-eight hours. Drain the water, rinse the kernels in a sieve and place in a large tray lined with moistened cotton and return to your warm dry spot. Ensure that the kernels are rinsed and the cotton wool is changed once a day. After four to five days the kernels will start to sprout. Once the sprouts are about double the size of the individual kernels, rinse them and leave them in a dry tray for twenty-four hours in a warm spot or on a window sill beneath direct sunlight.

Ingredients

500g *jora*
250g pearl barley
100g raw cane sugar
10l dechlorinated filtered water
packet of brewing yeast
2 cinnamon sticks
1 tbsp crushed coriander seeds

Equipment

Large cooking pot
Filtering equipment
Brewing bin
Earthenware jugs

Instructions

Pre-soak the pearl barley in cold water for twenty-four hours and drain well, leave to dry out for a further twenty-four hours. Lightly toast the *jora* and barley in oven trays over a low heat, shaking them regularly and transfer to the cooking pot. Use a stone pestle to mash up the *jora* and barley, add the water, sugar, yeast, cinnamon sticks and coriander seeds and cook on a low, bubbling heat for at least two hours, stirring regularly. Leave to cool until lukewarm and transfer to a sterilised brewing bin, cover and leave to stand for three to four days; agitate by stirring at least twice a day. Filter out the grains and other ingredients using filtering equipment such as sieves or cheesecloth straining bags. Transfer to pottery jugs and chill for a further two to three days before drinking (you may want to filter a second time to remove any further sediment).

Cheers!